Thank you for
your teaching!
In Christ,

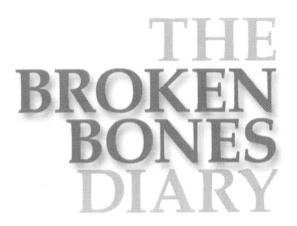

# THE BROKEN BONES DIARY

## HIS LIGHT IN MY DARKNESS

DIANA ESPEJO

WESTBOW
PRESS®
A DIVISION OF THOMAS NELSON
& ZONDERVAN

Scripture quotations taken from the New American Standard Bible® (NASB),
Copyright © 1960, 1962, 1963, 1968, 1971, 1972, 1973, 1975, 1977, 1995
by The Lockman Foundation.Used by permission. www.Lockman.org

This book is a work of non-fiction. Unless otherwise noted, the author
and the publisher make no explicit guarantees as to the accuracy of
the information contained in this book and in some cases, names of
people and places have been altered to protect their privacy.

WestBow Press books may be ordered through booksellers or by contacting:

WestBow Press
A Division of Thomas Nelson & Zondervan
1663 Liberty Drive
Bloomington, IN 47403
www.westbowpress.com
1 (866) 928-1240

Because of the dynamic nature of the Internet, any web addresses or
links contained in this book may have changed since publication and may
no longer be valid. The views expressed in this work are solely those
of the author and do not necessarily reflect the views of the publisher,
and the publisher hereby disclaims any responsibility for them.

Any people depicted in stock imagery provided by Thinkstock are
models, and such images are being used for illustrative purposes only.
Certain stock imagery © Thinkstock.

ISBN: 978-1-5127-8459-6 (sc)
ISBN: 978-1-5127-8460-2 (hc)
ISBN: 978-1-5127-8458-9 (e)

Library of Congress Control Number: 2017906443

Print information available on the last page.

Book design and artwork by Diana Espejo

WestBow Press rev. date: 06/05/2017

# DEDICATION

This book is dedicated to Theresa Attiogbe, my sister in Christ. God placed us in each other's lives for this very purpose. I remember the day you told me to write my journey down and turn it into a book. Thank you for tremendous spiritual fellowship and inspiration!

# PREFACE

It's hard to see God when things look fine. The majority of the time God has to break us down. We walk around in this world with our plans and our wills, and when they do not coincide with God's, He would rather break us in this time. However, He is the Great Healer, so whatever He breaks He heals.

That is exactly what happened to me that night when I realized who Jesus Christ was and that He came into my life because God loved me so much. God knew I needed help, He knew I needed a way out, and He showed me His glorious will for my life. Since then, it has been quite the ride, but God knows what He is doing.

We must trust Him. There is nothing else we can do if you humbly think about it. I hope this compilation of writings inspires you to obey God, read His Word, the Bible, and become more like Jesus Christ day by day. When this life is over, we will meet God face to face.

This is a diary that entails my spiritual journey, the diary of broken bones.

# CONTENTS

Make me to hear joy and gladness, Let the
bones which You have broken rejoice.

—Psalm 51:8

# CHAPTER 1

# GOD'S THOUGHTS ARE NOT OUR THOUGHTS

## May 16, 2011

"*I* would like May 11 through 14 off."

I got the time off, even though it was last minute. I can pretty much talk myself into getting whatever I want. The plan was to go visit my aunt from the Philippines whom I have not seen in decades. I asked my cousins in advance if it was okay to stay with them during those days. They said yes but to let them know for sure when I would be coming. Two months prior, the ticket price was $308 round trip, nonstop from Boston to Los Angeles. I did not buy that ticket because my cousins had to check to see if those dates would work for them. I missed out on a very low-priced fare, which irritated me. On May 2, I went hunting for the ticket again and found—*bam!*—$308, but the plane would fly into Santa Ana rather than the initially planned Los Angeles. I bought the ticket without consulting my cousins to make sure they would be able to pick me up from that airport. I then e-mailed my itinerary to them. They saw it was not what we planned and said, "We can't pick you up from that airport. We agreed when we last spoke that you should fly into Los Angeles." They also mentioned that they did not hear from me for weeks after I told them I would be going there, and that they were taking vacation on May 12.

"Who are you to tell me you can't pick me up from an airport that is merely twenty more minutes away? When I was ready to buy the ticket to Los Angeles, you would not call me back to confirm, and now you do not want to pick me up? The last time we spoke I clearly said May 11 to 14, and you planned your vacation for May 12—excuse me?"

Spoiled. For the first time, I did not get what I wanted.

Being spoiled is a clear sign of an ungrateful Christian. We have been given a wonderful package straight from God Himself once we choose to believe in the Lord Jesus Christ. This package has all the necessary equipment for us to walk and talk in this spiritual way of life called Christianity. Once we choose to put the equipment on, we then agree with the heart of this verse: "God's ways are not our ways; His thoughts are not our thoughts." (Isaiah 55:8–9).

Do you think God thinks like us? If He did, we would all be doomed! God doesn't think like us; check out how He decided to save the world, sending His one and only, His highest prized possession, to come down and become a human. He came from a place where time doesn't exist to a place where we revolve around time. He left heaven for earth. *Does this make any sense to anyone?* Yet it made all the sense to God. From the beginning, He had a plan intact, and it is playing out exactly how He designed it.

God is love. When I think of God, I have a glimpse of who and what He is because of His every word given to us (John 1:1), but when I think of love, my thoughts run wild.

What love do you want me to start with? Love at first sight? Love thy neighbor kind of love? Do you see how we humans think? He has to hit us hard, where only He knows it hurts to get our attention. Remember the Samaritan woman at the well, who was going for her "secret walk" up the "secret path" that she made to draw water so she would not be bothered by anyone around because she was labeled unwanted yet was the most talked about woman in town (John 4:5–42)? God had to hit home with her for her to understand His ways. He was telling her that He had water that would complete her life's thirst, and she was totally clueless. Then finally He hit her where it hurt, He brought up the dude.

"God's ways are not our ways; His thoughts are not our thoughts." If we put on the gear that came in the package, maybe we can see how God thinks. Put it on. Come on, you know you love opening gifts. Open the package and put that baby on! Try it out; let us see if the power works. Power? Yes, power!

> Seeing that His divine power has granted to
> us everything pertaining to life and godliness
> through the true knowledge of Him who
> called us by His own glory and excellence.
>
> —2 Peter 1:3

Wow! What a message from within the package. What is this package exactly? For the church or *ecclesia* (Greek word for "the called-out ones") the package consists of three unique powers, three in one, all in one. The Holy Trinity resides in all of us once we believe in our Lord and our Savior Jesus Christ. We have been sent this customized, special order from God Himself, drop shipped to our very own homes—no freight or taxes included, free of charge. Let us just call all of that grace. However, we must make the choice and put the power on. Have you taken inventory of how far your human power has taken you lately? Yeah, that is what I thought. Put it on.

"Whoa, who's that?" That is someone who doesn't know about this power. "What, you don't read the Bible? Really, it's the only way I'm still alive."

See what the power sees? It sees others in need of the power you have been given. It reveals to us God's thoughts. Our human thoughts slowly start to lose control of our minds. This power is powerful, people; you have to try it. This is not the latest fad on the market. This is the real deal. This is the power of all powers. With this power, selfishness becomes selflessness and we start to do things for others we never thought we would do.

Without the filling of the Holy Spirit, we are simply spoiled to think we are the best there is out there. Spoiled, little brats! Everything has to revolve around us. People need to cater to us. Jesus said, "I did not come to be served, but to serve" (Mark 10:45).

"God's ways are not our ways; His thoughts are not our thoughts." The result to my spoiled vacation was a $180 dollar loss, no vacation, and no seeing my aunt. Nevertheless, God used my negativity and turned it positive for me. I now know my spoiled weakness. I am aware of my lack of power. I am nothing without Christ.

"God's ways are not our ways; His thoughts are not our thoughts." Make some choices today. Did you say yes to the gift from God? Did you sign for the package? Is it sitting on the table unopened? Well, what are you waiting for? Open the package and put it on. Once you do, get ready, for you will get a glimpse of God Himself, satisfaction guaranteed.

# CHAPTER 2

# MISCALCULATIONS

## June 3, 2011

*M*ath was and still is my least favorite subject. Well, to be honest, I used to be good until the numbers started to have positive and negative signs before them. That threw me off— way off.

God designed women to be responders, and along with that design came the consequence of "a desire for a man" (Genesis 3:16). That sounds scary, huh? Well actually, that night was scary. I saw a side of me that I had never seen before: someone who threw principle out the door, someone who was hurting because of a guy and wanted to release the hurt with another guy, someone who was running from one relationship to the next.

Boy number one and I met online. We lived eight hours away from each other. He had a great personality, but I based him off of one picture. At the time, I had shallow eyes and he looked short, which was not my preference. We decided to meet in person, and he was definitely pretty short. I couldn't wear heels—let's just put it that way. After a few months of dating, it did not end too well. To keep things brief, he was one religion, I was another; his parents spoke one dialect, mine another; he was clingy, and I did not like clingy. I called him one day and said it wasn't going to work, after he pretty much told me that I was the girl he had been looking for his whole life. I crushed him. Miscalculation number one.

My relationship with boy number two can be defined in one word: karma. I fell hard for this one. He was everything I wanted in a guy, and then *I* became clingy. It appears he didn't like that, hence him changing his phone number when I told him I was coming to visit him a year after he broke up with me via the Internet while he was in Iraq. Maybe *clingy* is not the appropriate word to describe me at this point. I was extremely heartbroken. Miscalculation number two.

Still heartbroken, I met guy number three who was the complete opposite of me: he was involved in things I never cared for. He was a bit different from the rest, very outgoing, great date suggestions, something I wasn't used to. One day he asked me about my faith. Remember I am Catholic and Filipino, which is not a good mix for this type of conversation. He asked me questions that irritated me, but once it was said and done, they got me to think at night. Long story short, he ended up deploying to Iraq, and I ended up moving back to New York City. My emotions sort of went haywire when I first got to New York City, and I could not stop thinking about boy number two while I was in a long-distance relationship with boy number three. After a few months, I decided to break up with boy number three, which broke his heart. I needed to figure out why I could not stop thinking about boy number two. Miscalculation number three.

A few months went by. I was finally over boy number two, and unexpectedly I got a Bible in the mail from boy number three. It got me thinking again about all the questions he shook my faith with—questions left unanswered. Questions I ran away from without even knowing it. I remember a conversation we once had. It went something like this. "Do you believe in God?" "Yes." "Do you read the Bible?" "No, too skeptical of the authenticity of it." "Do you love God?" "Yes." "How can you love Him if you don't read the Bible? The Bible is the Word of God." Then I said something along the lines of, "Can you please leave me alone now?" He finally said, "Well if you love God, you should get to know Him."

This is the very statement that would eat at me while I was sitting in the second pew from the front of the church. My faith was something personal, something between God and me, and the questions kept coming. "Are you going to heaven?" Tears fell as I had no answer.

Looking back, I believe I cried because I did not have a clear answer to that question. I cried because it all came together. I really did not know who God was. I did not know in whom I believed. I did not know who I said I loved. Miscalculation number four.

Three boys later and I was still not happy; back to the scary night situation. As I walked out of the guy's apartment that morning, I actually did not feel guilty. I did not feel ashamed of my actions. I did not feel anything, and that was scary. Where did I go wrong? Why did my heart still hurt? Why wasn't life enjoyable as I thought when I was younger? Why was I making so much money, yet I was in debt? Why was I not learning about my Lord and Savior? Why do we recite "Holy Mary, mother of God" when it's not found in the Bible? Why does the priest say, "This is the Word of God" after his sermon, yet I was never really told to study His Word at church? Why did I stop trying to read the Bible when I was fourteen years old?

Why am I not married yet? Why does everyone think I am a great person, but I do not feel it? Where did I go wrong?

I miscalculated God. I put Him in a box. My life was full of worry, fear, and doubt and running away from unsolved mysteries. I filled the emptiness of my heart with everything and anything but God. I miscalculated God. I entered my digits into my manmade formulas and came up with my humanly reasoned estimation.

> Trust in the Lord with all your heart and
> do not lean on your own understanding.
>
> —Proverbs 3:5

Now that is simple math without the positive or negative before the numbers. "All" means God does all of it. That means God is the initiator of our salvation, and we are merely responders. He is the guy I have been looking for! He is the one who can solve my unformulated mathematical problem. He is the one who empowers us after salvation.

> Seeing that His divine power has granted to
> us everything pertaining to life and godliness
> through the true knowledge of Him who
> called us by His own glory and excellence.
>
> —2 Peter 1:3

*Everything* and *all*—these two words sum up what God takes care of.

> For you have been bought with a price;
> therefore glorify God in your body.
>
> —1 Corinthians 6:20

This life that we think is ours is not really ours. It's a life He has freely given us.

One last calculation, and before you try to solve it, remember the key word, *grace*. If in the beginning was the Word, and the Word was with God and the Word was God (John 1:1) and all scripture is God breathed (2 Timothy 3:16) and we have been made righteous, while as yet we were still sinners (Ephesians 2:5), then where do our calculations of ourselves and others fit in this God-breathed equation? Maybe we all need to chill out, stop analyzing, stop calculating, stop taking "sin notes," stop "fruit inspecting," and just let God work it all out. Look at what God's calculation ends up with:

And we know that God causes all things to work together for good to those who love God, to those who are called according to His purpose. (Romans 8:28)

God is a mathematical genius. I am all set with my miscalculations. It's time to surrender to the mathematical Genius who came up with this entire life equation and let Him solve it.

# CHAPTER 3

# HEARTACHE

## June 19, 2011

*If* only my dad would have made it to all my soccer games. If only I had a companion who was more sensitive to my needs. If only I got that position with that title. If only I had a better body. If only Adam did not listen to the woman when she offered him the forbidden fruit. If only, if only, if only. This reminds me of a popular song lyric, "I can't get no satisfaction."

An imputation means, "to attribute to" (in a bad sense) according to the *Webster's Dictionary,* 1987 edition. So what does this mean? Unfortunately, due to Adam's original sin, we received the consequences on the day of our physical birth and were born with an old sin nature.

"But how? I haven't even taken my first breath of life?" one may ask. Oh yeah, I know, I've asked the same thing, and sometimes I still can't wrap my head around the whole concept, but hopefully I can share a little glimpse of what God has revealed to me through my daily intake of His Word.

Let us venture into the beginning of the Bible and take

a closer look at what happened in Genesis 2:7. Adam was the first creation of humankind. You remember the infamous story, right? God did not deem it fit that Adam be alone, so He caused Adam to have a deep sleep and took one of his ribs (talk about a broken bone) and created the woman. The woman was deceived, ate of the tree of the knowledge of good and evil, and took it to her husband, and he ate. That is how it all started, my friends, and is the reason we all have a hole or a void in our hearts that can't be satisfied.

As soon as Adam and the woman ate of this forbidden fruit, they lost everything. They lost their love, patience, kindness, goodness, gentleness and started blaming one another. They lost their joy and faithfulness by hiding from God. They lost their peace; they saw they were naked and tried to hide. They lost their self-control and started making clothes out of fig leaves for crying out loud! They lost all the fruits of the Spirit.

That tree of the knowledge of good and evil distorted their vision from the tree of life. A veil now covered their spiritual eyes, and they could not see God clearly, nor hear or understand Him. They became aware of what *they* thought was good and what *they* thought was evil. Adam and the woman were in a perfect environment and were perfect for each other. God gave Adam bone of his bone, flesh of his flesh, the perfect woman for his life, yet it was not enough. They had access to only God knows how many trees, yet they wanted that one they could not have; the rest of the trees just weren't enough.

So why do we think we are any different? That job, that car, that man, that woman, that house, moving here, moving there, chasing that, filling the void in our hearts with anything and everything and yet still not enough. We are implacable, imperfect people. That is the very way He made us. Why? Well, He created us imperfect so that He could perfect us.

All of humankind is immersed in an ocean at birth. Picture this—some of us are good swimmers and will stay afloat for a while thinking we have everything in control, some of us mediocre swimmers and will soon tire out, and some will start to drown immediately. Bottom line, we were not made to swim continuously all our lives. We will eventually need someone to save us from drowning. This is a picture of our human strength. Now we must make a choice. We did not choose sin; Adam's sin was imputed to us. However, God offered us a choice to believe in Jesus Christ, the ultimate Lifeguard.

His ultimate love for us was the ultimate sacrifice of His One and Only Son, our Lord and Savior Jesus Christ, on whom God imputed all of our sin. He carried the cross without complaint, carried our sin graciously. He lived and died for the cross, and if we choose to believe in Him, we will be restored to our Father, Who is in heaven.

Allow Him to fill in that void with Himself so that after this life is said and done, you will be in the presence of the heavenly Father complete. He did everything for Adam and the woman. He continues to do everything for us, and the only thing any of His creations have to do, is choose to believe that He did. Once that happens, satisfaction takes place and the hole is filled.

> Give me your heart, my son, and let
> your eyes delight in my ways.
>
> —Proverbs 23:26

# CHAPTER 4

# DECEPTION, RESEARCH, TRUTH

## June 24, 2011

And without faith it is impossible to please
Him, for he who comes to God must
believe that He is and that He is a Rewarder
of those who diligently seek Him.

—Hebrews 11:6

There are questions that will not be answered in this lifetime, and you will have to humble yourself and accept it. If you are an analyzer like me, my advice to you is to do your research. Study the Word, pray to God for help, and see what He does to answer your efforts and prayers. This is exactly what I did, and my conclusion is He transforms a human's heart, not I. We are to be His ambassadors by putting on the Lord Jesus Christ (Romans 13:14). We are told to go and plant seeds (Matthew 28:19). God creates the growth. We plant and water (John 15:1–27). Present the Word of God to someone, and with his free will he will have to choose to accept.

If I could explain what happened to my soul once God revealed Himself to me, I would, but it's one of those things I can't really explain. I would leave too much out. All I know is it hurt and it still hurts, because a part of you, which you have honed, is falling apart, and you don't know what to do about it.

> He must increase, but I must decrease.
>
> —John 3:30

I hit rock bottom, but man, God's rock is solid and unshakeable.

> He only is my rock and my salvation, my
> stronghold; I shall not be greatly shaken.
>
> —Psalm 62:2

In my case, my rock bottom was where He was able to best minister to me. He was able to comfort me, because my heart was now open to the comforting. No two humans will have the same exact plan, and that's what makes His plan even more special. He has individualized plans for each and every one of us. That means we are unique in His eyes, and His eyes are all that matters.

Fear Him. That doesn't mean shake in your pants, because you sinned and you're guilty. The word *fear* in the Hebrew and Greek connotes reverence. Have reverence for Him. The Bible teaches us obedience is better than sacrifice.

> Has the LORD as much delight in burnt offerings
> and sacrifices as in obeying the voice of the
> LORD? Behold, to obey is better than sacrifice.
>
> —1 Samuel 15:22

Does this mean perfection? Absolutely not; it means power. It means that God has given you the power to execute His plan for your life. All we must do is rely on His power. How do we do this? We must read His GPS system: the Word of God. We must read what truly pleases Him.

My rock bottom was the fact that I deceived myself into thinking I could do something without my heavenly Father's strength and plan for my life. To me He was just a dead man's face in a picture frame I was praying to—someone over there out yonder, merely observing me from a distance. The Bible tells us He is in us, not merely watching us. He has provided us all with the Holy Spirit to execute this supernatural way of living.

> If you were of the world, the world would
> love its own; but because you are not of the
> world, but I chose you out of the world,
> because of this the world hates you.
>
> —John 15:19

My own little world was ripped apart before my very eyes. Everything I learned about God was ripped out, and nothing made any sense. That's when I had no other option but to get on my knees and pray. "What is it God? What is the truth? What is happening to me?" I wasn't aware of who I truly was because of His cross. I wasn't aware of where to get my instructions on how to live this life. When you read His Word, the deception will start to fade, and the truth will come forth.

> All Scripture is inspired by God and profitable for
> teaching, for reproof, for correction, for training

in righteousness; so that the man of God may
be adequate, equipped for every good work.

—2 Timothy 3:16–17

For the word of God is living and active
and sharper than any two-edged sword, and
piercing as far as the division of soul and spirit,
of both joints and marrow, and able to judge
the thoughts and intentions of the heart.

—Hebrews 4:12

In order for the truth to come forth, you must do your homework or research. I finally did, and it hurt because I was wrong. My pride hurt. As far as my pride knew, I was never wrong, but I was so wrong with this. My advice to those who are lost and confused or unbelieving is to do your research. God sees your efforts, and He said He will let you find Him if you seek Him with all your heart.

But from there you will seek the LORD your
God, and you will find Him if you search for
Him with all your heart and all your soul.

—Deuteronomy 4:29

Today there are numerous translations of the Bible, yet if you study the original languages in which the scriptures were written, what we have today is truly the Word of God. All the men who penned the Bible all experienced God's radical change in their lives. They went from nothing to something, by one common factor: having faith in Jesus Christ.

Many people possess the Bible, yet some are rarely opened.

If this book is the Word of God as it claims to be, why is it not being read every day?

> The grass withers, and the flower fades, but
> the Word of our God stands forever.

—Isaiah 40:8

These are some of the questions I was faced with. Do I know the one who loves me? Do I know the one who did everything for me? Do I know the one I say I trust in? Do I know what it meant for Him to come down from heaven and become a human to be sacrificed on the cross for humankind's sin? Do I know why He had to go to the cross? Does the church I belong to teach me about Him and His promises found in His word, or is it making me feel guilty? Do I know what I'm doing on this earth? Do I *want* to know these things?

> But I tell you that every careless word that
> people speak, they shall give an accounting
> for it in the Day of Judgment. For by
> your words you will be justified, and by
> your words you will be condemned.

—Matthew 12:36–37

To be completely honest with everyone, the majority of my answers to those in-your-face questions were no.

> Behold, I stand at the door and knock; if anyone
> hears My voice and opens the door, I will come in
> to him and will dine with him, and he with Me.

—Revelation 3:20

> Therefore the Lord longs to be gracious
> to you, and therefore He waits on high
> to have compassion on you. For the
> Lord is a God of justice; How blessed
> are all those who long for Him.

—Isaiah 30:18

It's never too late. You could be on your dying bed right now, withering away, and there is still enough time. Remember the thief on the cross? He was already nailed to the cross; he couldn't get down to walk to confession or to save the world by good deeds. He was hanging on the cross and couldn't leave that cross, yet he did the most important thing anyone could do in this lifetime; he turned to Jesus.

> But the other answered, and rebuking him said,
> "Do you not even fear God, since you are under
> the same sentence of condemnation? And we
> indeed are suffering justly, for we are receiving
> what we deserve for our deeds; but this man has
> done nothing wrong." Moreover, he was saying,
> "Jesus, remember me when You come in Your
> kingdom!" And He said to him, "Truly I say to
> you, today you shall be with Me in Paradise."

—Luke 23:40–43

Soak this in. The thief is now currently face to face with Jesus in an eternal state of perfection, because he believed in the one true power of the one true God. Let's say when we die, there is no judgment and there is no heaven or hell. I would still be able to say I lived this life to the fullest. Now let's believe the Word of God is actually true, precisely accurate, and there is a judgment, heaven, and hell? Is it really worth the time to just party, to simply work, to chase someone, or to pretend as if you can't hear the knock in your heart from your Creator? Is all that really worth your eternal state? I implore you to wake up. Start searching and being more aware of His presence that is with you before it's too late. I'm not trying to scare you; I just don't want you to have any regrets in this life. It's up to you to choose to do the research. Choose to wake up from your slumber, choose His power, and then see what happens next.

# CHAPTER 5

# YACHAL

## June 29, 2011

*W*e wait in line at the bank, at a drive-thru, for the newest cell phone, for that one person to make the first move, for our food once we order it; we are always waiting. But what is going on during the wait? How are we waiting? Are we tapping our feet in line or beeping at the person in front of us at the drive-thru? Do we actually really need that new cell phone, since the one we currently have works fine? Who are we waiting for, and how are we waiting?

*Yachal* is the Hebrew word "to wait expectantly." That means wait patiently and silently. This is not a maybe He won't or maybe He will definition. This is a without a doubt He is coming, inevitable expectation.

> Wait for the Lord; be strong and let your
> heart take courage; yes wait for the Lord.
>
> —Psalm 27:14

Wow, the word *wait* appears twice in one verse. That must mean something, a little emphasis maybe? God is telling us to take courage in Him and to be strong in Him.

> Therefore I am well content with weaknesses,
> with insults, with distresses, with persecutions,
> with difficulties, for Christ's sake; for
> when I am weak, then I am strong.

—2 Corinthians 12:10

> I can do all things through Him
> who strengthens me.

—Philippians 4:13

God is omnipotent, omniscient, and omnipresent. Simply put, He is all-powerful, all knowing, and everywhere all at once. He knows everything there is about each and every one of us: our surroundings and our circumstances.

> And there is no creature hidden from His
> sight, but all things are open and laid bare to
> the eyes of Him with whom we have to do.

—Hebrews 4:13

Three characteristics my old sin nature possess are all mental. I worry, fear, and doubt. So rather than reviewing the effects of these three characteristics (trust me, they are not fun), let's take a look at the cause. There is only one cause to all of our problems.

Let's take our imaginations to the ring, shall we? On one end, we have WFD (a.k.a., worry, fear, and doubt). On the other end is Three Os (a.k.a., omnipotence, omnipresence, and omniscience). Now that is what we call an unfair match. WFD can't outlast the Three Os. Let's look at who worry, fear, and doubt belong to. They belong to us. Now let's look at who the Three Os belong to. You got it, the King of the universe—the one who created everything.

> For by Him all things were created, both
> in the heavens and on earth, visible and
> invisible, whether thrones or dominions or
> rulers or authorities—all things have been
> created through Him and for Him.

> —Colossians 1:16

God's Three O characteristics can beat our WFD characteristics any day of the week. So, let's take the pressure off our shoulders, and wait for God to move in our lives. Now you're probably thinking, ok in order for me to wait that must mean I don't have to work, I'll just sit around and pray to God and He'll bring a gush of wind and pick me up off my sofa and take me places. No, remember we have free will, and with that comes the choice and ability to do something. It's about learning, understanding and then yes, we must do it, apply what we have learned. As one pretty famous company's slogan reads, "Just do it."

> The Lord is good to those who wait for Him,
> to the person who seeks Him. It's good that he
> waits silently for the salvation of the Lord.

> —Lamentations 3:25–26

I've memorized these verses so I can recite God's promises to myself when I can't sleep at night, if I'm on the road, while I'm stretching or taking a shower, or when everyone wants everything done yesterday at work, I recite them. God uses His words to comfort us and remind us that He is always a shout away. We really don't have to worry about anything anymore. The only way we can wait patiently and silently is if we know who is coming to our rescue or in correct terms, come to know *Who* has already rescued us. Then and only then can you truly wait patiently and silently for His presence in whatever situation you face at the moment.

CHAPTER **6**

# SHUT UP!

**June 31, 2011**

$\mathcal{M}$y dad's nickname for me when I was younger was "dal-dal." In Ilokano (a dialect of the Philippines) that means talkative. Oh yeah, I love to talk. I would literally talk about what shade of blue the sky was if someone would give me a chance!

The tongue is a great body part to have. It helps us to taste amazing spices—or lack thereof. It appreciates great flavors such as the green tea coconut gelato from Cold Fusion on a hot summer day in Newport, Rhode Island, or Malbec red wine on an upstate New York winter night, or the distinguished difference of the cashews at Daou Market in Fall River, Massachusetts. These are major, life-altering events for my tongue's history.

Along with every good thing God has provided for us, Satan, his crew, and of course, our old sin natures, have tried to corrupt them. We are capable of gossiping and maligning with our tongues. How many times have you said something without really thinking and afterward you wish you could take it back? For me, once my tongue gets started, it's very hard to stop. However, today something wild happened. My mouth didn't open after my ears heard something they didn't like. This is amazing news for Dal-dal! Gossiping was never my thing, but boy if I didn't like something I saw or if someone irritated me, I had no problem letting them know it. I could go on for days, resurrecting ancient history! I think it's safe to say I was a judge or an inspector of some sort. It was very easy for me to point out the wrong in others but not myself.

> Death and life are in the power of the tongue,
> and those who love it will eat its fruit.
>
> —Proverbs 18:21

> When there are many words, transgression is
> unavoidable, but he who restrains his lips is wise.
>
> —Proverbs 10:19

God had to wake me up. He said something along the lines of, "Hello, you do know that when you sin, you're not sinning toward anyone else but Me, right?" And He also told me that how I judge others will be the way He judges me. Ooh, that woke me up!

> Do not judge so that you will not be
> judged. For in the way you judge, you
> will be judged; and by your standard of
> measure, it will be measured to you.
>
> —Matthew 7:1–2

Jesus was spat upon, mocked by people, and told, "If You are the son of God, then save Yourself and us!" yet He didn't even open His mouth.

> He was oppressed and He was afflicted, yet He
> did not open His mouth; Like a lamb that is led
> to slaughter, and like a sheep that is silent before
> its shearers, so He did not open His mouth.
>
> —Isaiah 53:7

He didn't open His mouth! That's borderline unheard of today. No wait, that is unheard of today. I couldn't keep my mouth shut when my eyes saw something they didn't like, let alone someone mocking me. "Oh no they didn't" would be the start of that conversation.

The Bible says every believer will be conformed to Jesus Christ if only we choose to. He is our perfect example, not that we will ever become perfect here on earth but we are perfect in Christ. We are called sanctified, heirs of Christ—saints!

> I pray that the eyes of your heart may be
> enlightened, so that you will know what is
> the hope of His calling, what are the riches of
> the glory of His inheritance in the saints.
>
> —Ephesians 1:18

Once I realized the position I had with my Lord and Savior Jesus Christ, I carefully chose the things that came out of my mouth. I couldn't do it before, but now with the power of the Holy Trinity within me, I am capable of simply shutting up. There's no place for God's children to intentionally say things that hurt others. In the long run, we only end up hurting ourselves. If this has been a problem you have been facing, I pray God will also give you a glimpse as He did with me to allow you to zip it and learn how to control your tongue. You will need the power of His Word and the activation of the Holy Spirit to accomplish this.

# CHAPTER 7

# ONE OPTION

## July 9, 2011

*W*oman, such an intriguing creature. I'm hoping this will lend a helping hand to the ladies who have a problem with that certain week in the month. In my case, havoc is probably the best word to describe what happens to me when I go through this rollercoaster ride each and every month. Therefore I'm going to nickname it "Havoc." This is probably my number one question on my "Why God?" questions list when I get to heaven.

Scientifically it has been proven that a woman's hormone level changes immensely during this time, and therefore her emotions go haywire. In my case, it's starting to become this annoying song, like when the radio plays the same song over and over. It's to the point where I'm annoying myself, because I'm giving myself the same exact pep talk every month! My conclusion after all of the complaining and discussion with other women regarding this issue is summed up in this beautiful verse.

My grace is sufficient for you, for
power is perfected in weakness.

—2 Corinthians 12:9

God purposely created the female to be the weaker vessel. He knows why we go through what we go through every month and knows exactly how to comfort us during this time. I'm only twenty-seven, so I have years ahead of me before Havoc goes away, which I hear gives way to a whole other monster. I have no clue what I will name her.

My doctor recently asked me at my last checkup if I wanted a pill prescription to alleviate the emotional symptoms. I answered no, and the look on her face was priceless. She seemed to be in shock of my rapid answer to her routine question.

Most gladly, therefore, I will rather
boast about my weaknesses, so that the
power of Christ may dwell in me … for
when I am weak, then I am strong.

—2 Corinthians 12:9–10

The only option I had since I said no to the pill was to hand this over to God and give Him my pain, my tears, and my misunderstanding heart during this week. I must desperately cry out to Him.

So now, no longer am I the one doing it, but sin
which dwells in me. For I know that nothing
good dwells in me, that is, in my flesh; for the
willing is present in me, but the doing of the good
is not. For the good that I want, I do not do, but
practice the very evil that I do not want. But if
I am doing the very thing I do not want, I am

no longer the one doing it, but sin which dwells
in me … Wretched man that I am! Who will
set me free from the body of this death? Thanks
be to God through Jesus Christ our Lord!

—Romans 7:17–25

Jesus Christ is able and willing to change me during this time in preparation for eternity with Him in the high places.

All the fairest beauties in the human soul,
its greatest victories, and its most splendid
achievements are always those which no one
else knows anything about, or can only dimly
guess at. Every inner response of the human
heart to Love and every conquest over self-
love is a new flower on the tree of Love.

—*Hinds Feet in High Places,* Hannah Hurnard

God truly has one divine option in mind, and that is for us to have faith in Him, especially in our darkest moments. This is something that needs to be learned during our time on earth, and who better to learn it from than our Lord Jesus Christ. Havoc will cause me to self-destruct if I do not quickly hand it over to God. I can say I believe in Christ all day long, but if "Father knows best," then I must give Him full control over my life. I must read His Word consistently, or else there will be constant room for our flesh to wreak havoc at any moment.

# CHAPTER 8

# AN OBEDIENT, REVERENT RESPONSE

## July 16, 2011

*I* remember my father waking us up Saturday mornings by blasting Cool and the Gang's song "Celebration." What were we celebrating exactly? I guess in my dad's world, Saturday morning chores, whoopee! I deep down inside, enjoyed it. I like the whole concept of a family coming together to clean the whole house. My dad was more than likely using the disciplinary skills he learned in the military to create his *own* soldiers (ha, ha).

Discipline—this is a word that one can take out of context really quick. A lot of people view discipline as a negative action. I never quite looked at it that way when I was younger. I always took the view of, "my father knows what's best for me as of this point in my life." I can only imagine what it would be like to be ten years old, without any sense of direction. I thank my father and mother for giving me that direction. In my eyes, discipline is like direction or guidance. The more disciplined we are, the better off we will be when we move out of the house. I believe that was my parents' view on discipline. It's no surprise to me that that is how the Bible portrays discipline.

> Furthermore, we had earthly fathers to discipline us, and we respected them; shall we not much rather be subject to the Father of spirits, and live? For they disciplined us for a short time as seemed best to them, but He disciplines us for our good, so that we may share His holiness.
>
> —Hebrews 12:9–10

God the Father is our true Guidance Counselor. His Son Jesus Christ left heaven to lay down His life to rescue us from our sin. Now a lot of us don't think we have sin. Many of us have done an excellent job of hiding our sins overtly, but inwardly, it doesn't look pretty. The true nature can be hidden from time to time, as well as long periods, but ultimately, it will burst out, like a time bomb. Let's face it; we would never discipline ourselves given the opportunity. We are so arrogant or ignorant that we don't think we need help. We think we can do it all on our own until—*bam!*—maybe the one human being you gave your heart to disappoints you, better yet breaks your heart by cheating, or gives up on the relationship. Maybe a disease takes place in your body and makes you extremely sick. Maybe you just bought a house, then lost your job. Maybe a member of your family turns on you; maybe he or she just stops answering the phone. Maybe someone really close to you passes away, a person you looked up to and respected. Rather than asking what you did wrong to deserve the situation, going out to seek revenge on whatever the issue may be, or having self-pity on yourself that things are unfair in your life, try stopping and seeking His Word for guidance. Sometimes God has to wake us up from our "sleep" or our nonchalant stages in life. It's like the smack on the butt with the belt from the dad who wants to show you that you can't keep doing what you're doing, or acting how you're acting. It's like the "you're grounded, go to your room" speech. It's like the slap on the thigh, leaving a horrific bruise moment.

With our free will we have the ability to pretty much do what we set our minds on doing. However, God, being a just God, will allow us to go through certain paths that will hopefully wake us up, and make us look up and start to seek Him.

> I must tell you that this precipice to which the
> path has led you is at the foot of Mount Injury.
> The whole mountain range stretches a long way
> beyond this in either direction, and everywhere
> it's as steep or even steeper than here. There are
> even more terrible precipices on the other sides
> of Mount Reviling and Mount Hate and Mount
> Persecution and others besides, but nowhere
> is it possible to find a way up to the High
> Places and into the Kingdom of Love, without
> surmounting at least one of them. This is the
> one which I have chosen for you to ascent.

> —*Hinds Feet on High Places,* Hannah Hurnard

Before our father and mother even thought of creating us, God knew us, and He had in mind the best plan for us. In Much-Afraid's case in the book *Hinds Feet on High Places,* God chose her to surmount Mount Injury. We all think things are better on the other side, "if only I was born elsewhere" or "had better parents," etc. We all have our own mountains to climb, allowed by God Himself, and no two mountains are alike by any means. We must seek the One who created the mountain to get our direction for the climb.

I have been led to cut out certain things in my life for certain periods of time. I haven't watched television since October 2010. Why, one may ask? "Is it because you think television is bad for Christians?" Definitely not. I know myself, and I know I must seek His advice for the best route up this mountain, and the television was a hindrance. Clothing ads, romantic comedy shows, talk show nonsense, and reality contests have no help in guiding me or giving me encouragement for my eternal state. It only gives me hours to be conformed to this world, rather than hours of being transformed by the renewing of my mind. I had to turn it off, and I must say it feels good to unload that unnecessary bondage I chose to be in.

Facebook, oh Facebook. I used to be a Facebook fanatic. I used to post anything cool I saw or thought of, and I enjoyed the whole concept of keeping in touch with everyone. I was able to express what I referred to as my "talents" back then. The more accurate word was my self-centeredness. I closed that door fast and haven't looked back.

*Self, Cosmopolitan, Fitness, Glamour, Vogue, Shape, Lucky.* The latest and greatest fashion statements, the newest color to wear, the best places to have sex, different tricks to make a guy go crazy, the healthiest food of the year, all the shopping deals in the world! That's what I was conforming my mind to. I mean, seriously I had magazines from 2001 that I kept because of certain health articles, workouts, or pictures that I liked a lot, all nonsense. I had to make a choice to throw them out. I used to donate them by leaving them in a public area, but this time around, I threw them out because I didn't even want to condone anyone else to seek the advice from those magazines.

"Why? Are you not strong enough, Diana? You can't handle a little hour of talk show nonsense? You can't stand a magazine article? You can't stand the socialness of the Internet realm?"

> There is a way which seems right to a
> man, but its end is the way of death.
>
> —Proverbs 16:25

> Therefore be careful how you walk, not as
> unwise men but as wise, making the most
> of your time, because the days are evil.
>
> —Ephesians 5:15–16

God once asked Solomon to pray for anything he wanted. Do you recall what Solomon asked for? If you consider yourself a disciple, this should be a part of your daily prayer.

> In Gibeon the Lord appeared to Solomon
> in a dream at night; and God said "Ask
> what you wish Me to give you."
>
> —1 Kings 3:5

> So give Your servant an understanding
> heart to judge Your people to discern
> between good and evil.
>
> —1 Kings 3:9

We need understanding and discernment of why we are here and what we are to do in our time. If God did the greatest He could for us by sending His Son Jesus Christ, our Lord and Savior, to pay the ultimate price for our eternal salvation, then how are we to respond to this great act of grace? Oh, how simple it is to go the way of everyone else—to do what they tell you is cool or in at the moment. The easy way is to simply fit in with the rest of the world, right? However, God tells us otherwise. We are not of this world.

> For our citizenship is in heaven, from which also
> we eagerly wait for a Savior, the Lord Jesus Christ.
>
> —Philippians 3:20

God brought me to a point where my actions needed to match with my words. Here I was, preaching the good news of Christ to all my friends and family, yet I myself was not walking with Him. I was not reading His word on a daily basis, seeking the things of His kingdom or His calling upon my life. I was spending my time on Facebook, reading unreal magazines and watching Hollywood excel at worthless drama. I am now starting to understand that I am a child of God. I am not to be conformed to this world. His discipline in our lives is for our own benefit. Consider yourselves lucky to have parental discipline in preparation for life without constant instruction. God does it even more and with far more significance.

> My son, do not reject the discipline of the
> Lord or loathe His reproof, for whom the
> Lord loves He reproves, even as a father
> corrects the son in whom he delights.
>
> —Proverbs 3:11–12

If you have heard God's calling to your life as an ambassador for Him, accept it and so walk in it.

# CHAPTER 9

# HOW GREAT IS YOUR DARKNESS?

## July 30, 2011

*W*hen you think you can do it on your own, you are in the deepest form of deception. If you think you are able to accomplish anything in this life without God's power, you are in the midst of destruction.

I speak from empiricism. I definitely had a love for God at a very young age. I remember the hassle of trying to wake everyone up so we could be on time for the 11:00 a.m. service on Sundays when I didn't drive yet. I remember jumping in the car by 10:45 a.m. thinking to myself that I couldn't wait to get a car because I would never be late for church. I wanted to be on time for God. I always knew God was watching me, and I tried to please Him. I lived in a phase where I was doing things my way, calling all the shots. This started at a very young age.

In my case, I got exactly what I wanted, but there was still emptiness in my heart and I couldn't stop but wonder why my heart wasn't satisfied. I was living in New York City, in my opinion the greatest city in the United States. I was working in the fashion industry, making $50,000 a year at the mere age of twenty-two, which was much higher than the average twenty-two-year-old that year. I was hustling and bustling, relying on what my eyesight told me was right. Work hard, retire early, and life will be groovy. Why wasn't I fulfilled, New York? Why wasn't I satisfied with a $50,000 salary at the age of twenty-two? Why did something in my heart, mind, body, and soul still thirst?

Truthfully looking back, I was not happy. I couldn't even discern that I was going down a road that led to wreckage. Why? Because I didn't know. Why didn't I know? I wasn't told. Then I was told, but I still didn't *know*. Why not? Because I didn't want to listen.

These were questions that would taunt me over and over. My "mine, mine, mine" bubble was popping, and I didn't like it. I spent so much of my time building this bubble that I walked in. It was reassuring.

> If then the light that is in you is
> darkness, how great is the darkness!
>
> —Matthew 6:23

It was like God was speaking this whole time, but I couldn't hear Him because of all the nonsense I placed around me. All of the clothes, fancy restaurants, lights, camera, and action came tumbling down. I thought God was supposed to make everything peachy as long as I went to church. This was darkness, but I thought it was light until I started reading the Word of God.

> I love those who love Me; and those who
> diligently seek me will find Me.
>
> —Proverbs 8:17

> You will seek Me and find Me when you
> search for Me with all your heart.
>
> —Jeremiah 29:13

When you start to seek God with all your heart, soul, mind, and strength, it may not appear normal to the world. Reading the Bible trained me to see what His grace and love was truly about. I was excited about this new chapter of my life. However, the ride for a Christian is never smooth. It was like God drove me into chaos. My life was filled with heartache, loneliness, anger, bitterness, pain, and misery. On the outside, I looked great, but my insides were a mess.

God crumbled my whole life that I spent years fabricating. He stopped everything and crumbled all the clay to build something totally new. All of my norms and standards were thrown out the door. What He did I can never forget. What I know is He made me brand new. The power I had growing up experienced a brutal death filled with misery and heartache. Now I am operating with a far greater power because it's His power within me.

# CHAPTER 10

# KEEP GOING

## August 20, 2011

"*O*nce saved, always saved." If you are a Christian, you recognize what this statement means. If you aren't, well, it simply means that once you believe in the Lord Jesus Christ you are eternally saved no matter what happened before that moment or what will happen after. Once you believe in Jesus Christ, you get an e-ticket into heaven. The ticket can't be stolen or taken back. It simply lives in the system forever. What's next once this beautiful awakening happens? Do you go back to the way you were acting and thinking before you understood Who Jesus Christ was and what He did for you? Is that really the smart thing to do?

> For all have sinned and fall short
> of the glory of God.
>
> —Romans 3:23

In blatant terms, we are bad. To make you feel better, we are all equally bad. Great news for us, right? Therefore, no one should compare and contrast each other's sins. Salvation is best described in the following verse.

> For by grace you have been saved through faith;
> and that not of yourselves, it is the gift of God;
> not as a result of works, so that no one may boast.
>
> —Ephesians 2:8–9

Grace is the best definition for salvation. My pastor's definition for grace is that we don't earn or deserve it. God's grace saved all of us by sending His Son Jesus Christ from heaven to walk on this earth. He became like us to die for us. He died because of sin. Sin is a blockage in our lives, and Jesus paid for our sins. After salvation, we have the choice to walk with Him. We can walk in His ways and strive to obey Him. He did all of this for us so we could have hope.

> For the wages of sin is death, but the free gift
> of God is eternal life in Christ Jesus our Lord.
>
> —Romans 6:23

He was born to die for us, and now He is in us, so we have the power to walk in Him. This is what should happen after salvation. Walk and persevere. We are going to continue to fall, but we must keep going!

> I press on toward the goal for the prize of
> the upward call of God in Jesus Christ.
>
> —Philippians 3:14

## KEEP GOING

Let us also lay aside every encumbrance and
the sin which so easily entangles us, and
let us run with endurance the race that is
set before us, fixing our eyes on Jesus.

—Hebrews 12:1–2

# CHAPTER 11

# HELPLESS BUT NOT HOPELESS

## August 28, 2011

*I*'m sitting on my couch looking out the window, ankle iced and raised on three pillows, making sure it's higher than my heart per the doctor's instructions. I'm watching as Hurricane Irene washes my car and everyone else's. This verse comes to my mind.

> So the helpless has hope.
>
> —Job 5:16

This is a great image of humankind. We can't help ourselves even if we wanted to. I sprained my ankle a month ago, and there's nothing I can do to make it heal any faster than it has been healing. I could elevate it the whole day, but it still wouldn't heal from the inside overnight, or in my timing.

Many families right now are desiring to go somewhere, but even if they wanted to, they wouldn't be able with these severe weather conditions. Humankind in our naturalness, in our flesh so to speak, can't do anything about our wickedness. We are helpless in and of ourselves. If we can't help ourselves, how can we possibly help anyone else who is in the same condition?

I was listening to a radio broadcast today, and the pastor said he wakes up every morning acknowledging the fact that he is able to sin. Because he is able to sin today, that brings him right to his knees. What a sober assessment of our natural state as humans. We all should wake up and acknowledge our wickedness, because sin is sin to God. The result of sin is all the same.

For the wages of sin is death.

—Romans 6:23

So now what? What can we do? If we can't help ourselves, and we can't help anyone else in this matter, then what do we do? I'm sure everyone has heard of a man named Jesus Christ, right? This name has been under attack more than any other name that has ever faced this planet. Jesus Christ, Superstar. He was a human who was able not to sin. He came down as 100 percent human and 100 percent deity. He was made sin on our behalf and was sacrificed to God, fulfilling the Jewish laws of sacrificial offerings for sins. Therefore, His completed work on the cross saved us. Dying, He saved us.

By the end of this night, Hurricane Irene is going to do a lot of damage. Trees will be down, power will be lost, streets will be flooded, and eventually people will start to get sick. Now picture a rescue worker coming to the scene and picking people up, lifting them up from the waste, the tragedy. That is exactly our state as humans before we believe in Jesus. The King of kings and the Lord of lords came down from heaven to help once and for all. All we have to do is reach out for His hand, and He will pick us up. He will adopt us and give us beautiful clothes, crowns and jewels. As He is a king, we become royalty when He picks us up.

> But you are a chosen race, a royal priesthood,
> a holy nation, a people for God's own
> possession, so that you may proclaim the
> excellencies of Him who has called you out
> of darkness into His marvelous light.

—1 Peter 2:9

> And if children, heirs also, heirs of
> God and fellow heirs with Christ.

—Romans 8:17

Who wants to stay in a tragedy? Who wants to stay in a state of depravity? Who wants to stay behind? If you have never heard the gospel, well now you have. Make a choice. If you have heard the gospel, whether it was from a friend, a family member, or even a stranger, make a choice. If you have heard the gospel and have accepted Christ as your Savior, you have a daily choice to walk with Him today. His royal hands are reaching for you; reach back. The sooner you can look at yourself and admit you can't help yourself, the sooner you allow Christ to pick you up. This life will have new meaning the moment you can admit you are a sinner. Reach out. We are helpless, yet not hopeless. Jesus Christ is our true hope.

> But God demonstrates His own love toward us, in
> that while we were yet sinners, Christ died for us.

—Romans 5:8

# CHAPTER 12

# CRACKS

**September 12, 2011**

God has been on a testing spree with me lately, and I have failed every single one. My retake exam is in roughly one month. Please say a prayer for me.

I was driving home last night and a pastor on the radio spoke about being sincere in our faith to Jesus. Lately, I've been keeping a dictionary by my bed to look up a lot of the words found in the Bible. Even the words I think I know, I look up, because sometimes we become too familiar with words and we start to turn them into our own definitions and it's good to rediscover the true meaning.

"Sincere—adj: not assumed or merely professed; straight forward. Noun: a state or quality of being sincere, honesty of mind or intention; truthfulness."[1]

The pastor was explaining that we must be sincere with our relationship to Christ. He said that many say they believe,

---

[1] *Webster's Dictionary*, 1987 ed., s.v. "sincere."

but few sincerely trust. To be sincere myself, as of right now, I can't say I fully trust Him with everything, yet. But God is still working in me and all of us until the day He calls us home.

Another pastor I was listening to spoke about suffering today and how God uses it to "adjust" us. This reminded me of my appointments with the chiropractor. Here we are out of the womb: we live a little, grow a little, and because of our free wills, our very muscles and tendons bend in certain ways. I never stood up straight when I was a teenager, so I had poor posture, and I'm still paying for it today. Sometimes when we don't go to God for certain things, or with certain areas of our lives that need adjusting, we get used to them. We leave those rooms in our souls unattended, or maybe screaming for help, but we don't hear it because it has now become normal to us. Then God comes in and starts to adjust, and it hurts, because we aren't used to it. Although He knows and later we will agree that that very hurt or adjustment was for our own good. At times, He uses hurt to strengthen us.

E. G. White writes in her book *Character Construction*, "Trials and obstacles are the Lord's chosen methods of discipline and His appointed conditions of success. He who reads the hearts of men knows their characters better than they themselves know them. He sees that some have powers and susceptibilities which, rightly directed, might be used in the advancement of His work."[2]

"Power—capacity for action, physical, mental, or moral; energy; might; agency or motive force; authority; one in authority; influence or ascendancy; a nation; mechanical

---

[2] E. G. White, *Character Construction* (Pacific Press Publishing Association, 2011).

energy. The product arising from the continued multiplication of a number by itself."[3]

I like the last definition from the dictionary. It's like a math equation: "the product arising from the continued multiplication of a number by itself."[4]

Once we believe in Jesus, we are given His very power. He indwells us, and therefore we become Christ-like, and there are Jesuses everywhere. Yes, He is seated at the right hand of God right now, but He also resides in all believers. He has multiplied Himself in us.

> Not that we are adequate in ourselves
> to consider anything as coming from
> ourselves, but our adequacy is from God.
>
> —2 Corinthians 3:5

"Susceptibility—capable of; readily impressed; sensitive, receptive."[5]

"He sees that some have powers and susceptibilities which, rightly directed ..." Rightly directed: our goal is to bring glory to God during our time here on earth and our time is very minimal. God gave us different talents. With those talents, power and susceptibilities we must learn to use them to bring Him glory; we must learn to direct them to Him. "He sees that some have powers and susceptibilities which, rightly directed, might be used in the advancement of His work."

The pastor I was listening to assured me to examine myself.

---

[3] *Webster's Dictionary*, 1987 ed., s.v. "power."

[4] Ibid.

[5] *Webster's Dictionary*, 1987 ed., s.v. "susceptibility."

Am I truly, sincerely in love with Christ my Lord? He then provided a visual aid. An expensive, handmade vase, if cracked, on the outside, can be repainted with color and a coat of gloss, and to the human eye the crack wouldn't be visible. But in the inside the crack is known and visible to the artist. God is the artist.

Is your vessel cracked? Mine is. I've repainted it numerous times, and I've even put a shiny gloss over it so that no one else can see the cracks. But *the* Artist sees my cracks, and He keeps knocking at my "soul doors" with all these messages by different pastors, people I don't even know, and songs on the radio. He is knocking, using everything and anything to get my attention. He got it for the three hundredth time last night, and so I'm turning to Him to fix them, all of them, one by one, in His timing, not mine. He has warned me several times that He will fix, heal, repair, and adjust my cracks in His timing alone. That is the deal He has made with me.

From one cracked vessel to another, examine yourself and go to the throne of God privately with your imperfections and surrender them to Him. He loves each and every one of us, and He knows better than we do. Give them to His care and trust that He will make them better in His time.

> And we know that God causes all things to work
> together for good to those who love God, to
> those who are called according to His purpose.
>
> —Romans 8:28

# CHAPTER 13

# BIRTHDAYS

## October 11, 2011

*T*wenty-eight years of age. Man oh man, that is a long time.

> For this reason, I say to you, her sins, which
> are many, have been forgiven, for she loved
> much; but he who is forgiven little, loves little.
>
> —Luke 7:47

This verse sums up this past year nicely for me. Max Lucado, in his book *A Love Worth Giving*, describes this verse as the woman who "crashed Simon the Pharisee's party" and washed Jesus's feet with her tears and her "highest prized possession," her alabaster vial of perfume.[6]

This past year I have experienced "Simon the Pharisee" turning slowly into the woman. How? Because the older you get, the wiser you get if you continue in His Word. It has been such a realization period of how condemned I was before I

---

[6] Max Lucado, *A Love Worth Giving* (Thomas Nelson, 2009).

finally knew who Jesus was and what He did for me, and for all of us. Out of the twenty-seven years of my life, only one so far has been a year where I have been loving God with all my heart, soul, and strength (Deuteronomy 6:5). I recognize years in quantity do not count. However, it's a nice reminder of where you once came from. I do not mean nationality or geography; I mean who I was back then. My character: things I once lived for, the things that pained me, and the things that made me smile.

Birthdays have a way to force us to reflect, well for me at least, and this birthday is already special. The reflections of the past year have been phenomenal. I know I have not reached anything per say, but I know I have made some big faith jumps, all because of Who He is. His grace, His Word, His mind, and His love are amazing and unfathomable.

> Oh, the depth of the riches both of the wisdom
> and knowledge of God! How unsearchable are
> His judgments and unfathomable His ways!
>
> —Romans 11:33

Looking back, a piece of His mind comes to my mind. He used the apostle Paul to testify and write the following about who he used to be, before he met Christ:

> Although I myself might have confidence, even
> in the flesh. If anyone else has a mind to put
> confidence in the flesh, I far more; circumcised
> the eighth day, of the nation of Israel, of the tribe
> of Benjamin, a Hebrew of Hebrews, as to the
> Law, a Pharisee; as to zeal, a persecutor of the
> church; as to the righteousness which is in the
> Law, found blameless. But whatever things were

gain to me, those things I have counted as loss
for the sake of Christ. More than that, I count
all things to be loss in view of the surpassing
value of knowing Christ Jesus my Lord, for
whom I have suffered the loss of all things,
and count them but rubbish so that I may gain
Christ, and may be found in Him, not having
a righteousness of my own derived from the
Law, but that which is through faith in Christ,
the righteousness which comes from God on
the basis of faith, that I may know Him and the
power of His resurrection and the fellowship of
His sufferings, being conformed to His death; in
order that I may attain to the resurrection from
the dead. Not that I have already obtained it or
have already become perfect, but I press on so
that I may lay hold of that for which also I was
laid hold of by Christ Jesus. Brethren, I do not
regard myself as having laid hold of it yet; but
one thing I do; forgetting what lies behind and
reaching forward to what lies ahead, I press on
toward the goal for the prize of the upward call of
God in Christ Jesus. Let us therefore, as many as
are perfect, have this attitude, and if in anything
you have a different attitude, God will reveal
that also to you; however let us keep living by
that same standard to which we have attained.

—Philippians 3:4–16

I actually thought at one period of my life that I was in
control and that I can do everything I set my mind to if I work
hard enough. Boy was I wrong. Jesus was sent on our behalf
to pay the penalty of our sins. He is God, He did not have to
leave heaven to come down to be born of a virgin, and He

did not do it for kicks. He was sent by God because that's how much God loves us. He gave His only begotten Son to die for us, and that's how much we have been forgiven. God gave Jesus, our Lord and our Savior, to take all the sins of the world away. I and everyone else who chooses to believe Him has been forgiven much. If we can truly digest that forgiveness that took place from the day Jesus Christ was born, to the finishing work of His cross for our sins and wretchedness, then we can love much. We are then able to love in this order: God, ourselves, and others. This is a commandment from God. This is what we ought to do if we call ourselves disciples. This characteristic has been imputed to us the day we believed in Jesus Christ. This is His nature, and by His grace we can partake of it. We can't unconditionally love without realizing that God loved us first. Because God forgave me much, I am now able to love everyone in return in reverence to His love. Nevertheless, this is something learned. As my pastor puts it: love is a system of thinking. For the majority of us, we have to change our thinking first. We do this by handing over the power we think we have, in exchange of the true power freely given from God, and all you have to do is accept it and learn the way He thinks. When you love God personally, then and only then can you have impersonal love for everyone else. I pray that I will have another year of loving the Lord with all of my heart, soul, and strength, in return developing a love for all humanity. By His power, and His power only, it can be achieved.

But with God all things are possible.

—Matthew 19:26

# CHAPTER 14

# ACTION!

## November 5, 2011

$\mathcal{W}$e all know one, or maybe we are the one—the person who finds something to say in every moment of silence. The one who keeps talking when no one is listening. I once subtly asked a friend who fit this bill why it was that he could never keep quiet. To my shock, he said, "It's too quiet. It doesn't feel right."

Many people talk to simply fill in the silence. Unfortunately, that is how many Christians are today. We all talk. I say we, because I am no different. I read the Bible daily, I say my prayers, I go to church to learn more about my Lord and Savior, but when the going gets tough—then what? It's comparable to students going through college. The professors are teaching them all the book knowledge they will never need to know. Nine out of ten times they will learn by experience. When I was a student, I was ready to go out to the "real world," but then when I got there, I wanted to go back to school!

Look at Peter, he walked with Jesus, he talked with Jesus,

he believed Jesus was the Christ, but when the rooster crowed that third time, Peter was in denial. Peter was watching from a distance as they brought Christ to the high priests and elders. He was trying to warm himself, Mark points out (Mark 14:54, 67). What about the infamous bed sheet dude who was following Jesus, covered in linen, but when the soldiers seized him, he escaped naked (Mark 14:51)? He left his blanket of faith. He wanted to spare himself, even if it meant him running about naked. How many of us do the same thing? We say "praise the Lord" one day, but we get "seized" by the world because of who we believe in the next day. When God feels like putting us through test after test after test, we simply give up.

> Consider it all joy, my brethren, when you
> encounter various trials, knowing that the
> testing of your faith produces endurance.

> —James 1:2

> For just as the sufferings of Christ are
> ours in abundance, so also our comfort
> is abundant through Christ.

> —2 Corinthians 1:5

We need to rejoice when we have the chance to apply everything we have learned and profess. Therefore, when Jesus tells us to do something difficult, or when He puts us through something difficult, we better be ready to go with Him. Sometimes I think what could have happened with Peter had he stayed with Christ. Would he have ministered to Christ's humanity by being by His side? Would he have been able to give the gospel out to some of the elders? None of that really matters now, because all things happen for good to those who love God, but it's something to think about the next time you find yourself being tested by Him. Besides, without that low tide Peter would have never penned 1 Peter and 2 Peter the way we read them today.

The wonderful thing is that God knows all of us with every minute detail, and knows the best tests for each of us individually. Now that we have access to the completed Bible, we ought to learn from the things that happened to the apostles and disciples. If Christ is Lord of all, and trouble appeared and we separated from Him, can we honestly say we are safe? Aren't we safer through the trials with Christ, rather than alone? Doesn't His word say He will never leave us nor forsake us (Deuteronomy 31:6)? Doesn't His word say we can do all things through Christ who gives us strength (Philippians 4:13)? Then why is it that we run away right when a test is coming? Typically, after a test passes, a blessing is right around the corner. I like to think the test *is* the blessing, and if we pass the test, we gain greater capacity for a bigger test. Yikes, I know that is scary! What else are you going to do with me God? All the while He is saying, "Oh, there is plenty that needs to be done. Just enjoy the ride—I mean life."

In heaven, this will all make sense to us. It may not seem so masterful now, but patience is a fruit of the Spirit for a reason. We need to wait patiently and silently for His deliverance in all areas of our lives. Let Him get us through the painful heartache of losing a loved one or losing a much-needed job. Allow Him to guide us in our decision making.

For our citizenship is in heaven, from which also
we eagerly wait for a Savior, the Lord Jesus Christ.

—Philippians 3:20

Do not get too comfortable down here, for this is not our home. Do not be conformed to this world while here, but be transformed (Romans 12:2). It's like that fantasy movie when the superhero comes from a different planet and then falls in love with a human with the thought of staying forever. May that never be for us. Rather we must stay on the alert, because Satan wants us to get comfortable here. He wants us to enjoy the things of this world, to the point where it hinders our spiritual walk and relationship with Christ. He wants us to believe his lying whispers that we are not ambassadors and that we are just helpless guinea pigs that have no say in anything.

> Be of sober spirit, be on the alert. Your adversary, the devil, prowls around like a roaring lion, seeking someone to devour.

> —1 Peter 5:8

The only way to conquer all of this is found in the following two verses. There are so many, but these two have spoken to me this past month:

> But seek first His kingdom and His righteousness, and all these things will be added to you.

> —Matthew 6:33

> Finally, brethren, whatever is true, whatever is honorable, whatever is right, whatever is pure, whatever is lovely, whatever is of good repute, if there is any excellence and if anything worthy of praise, dwell on these things.

> —Philippians 4:8

## ACTION!

This is how we are going to return home, as superheroes. We must keep our souls fixed, focused, and in tune with our Lord and Savior. Never forget your inheritance with Christ. Never forget your human status: we are all sick, we all need help, and we definitely can't help ourselves. Jesus is the only One who can help, especially when the going gets tough.

> Therefore I run in such a way, as not without aim; I box in such a way, as not beating the air; but I discipline my body and make it my slave, so that, after I have preached to others, I myself will not be disqualified.

> —1 Corinthians 9:26–27

# CHAPTER 15

# I USED TO DATE DESTRUCTION

### December 4, 2011

"*Y*ou can't do it." "It will never happen for you." "Stop trying and just give up on God." "God, who is He and why is He making you suffer?" "Look at your brother—he has it all, and you have nothing!" "You will never get married. You will end up alone!" "Everything you get involved in never works out." "You ruin everything!"

Drowning. I am drowning, because of all the invisible attacks. Where are they coming from? Why must I hear them? How can I stop them from repeating the same things constantly?

We all have it: the evil nature within. In God's Word, it's called the "old self." It's the nature that produces the comments above, the nature that tries to do good but can't. This nature is nothing other than evil. A friend once asked me what the purpose of the Ten Commandments were. As stated in God's Word, it was used as a tutor of sin. It taught the nations what sin was. If you don't know what is wrong, how will you know what is right, right?

> Therefore did that which is good become a
> cause of death for me? May it never be! Rather
> it was sin, in order that it might be shown to be
> sin by affecting my death through that which
> is good, so that through the commandments
> sin would become utterly sinful.

—Romans 7:13

When Jesus came, He satisfied the Ten Commandments and fulfilled their significance. The old self was then crucified with Jesus's body on the cross. How can we live with double natures within us? If you believe in Jesus Christ, the one who closed the gap between God and humankind, then you have experienced a resurrection in this life. A new life has emerged. Something new has replaced the old. When Christ rose, the Holy Spirit came forth and now lives in everyone who believes in Him. However, on earth our flesh is the casing of our old self and will be present until the casing dies. But once the Holy Spirit resides in you, you can operate with the new self. The old self will no longer have power, unless you choose to press its buttons so to speak.

Ever since I have been diving into the Word of God, God shows me yet another repulsive room in my soul that needs His cleaning. At times, I often ask myself, "Wow, is this how you've always been, and just didn't know it?"

> For what I am doing, I do not understand;
> for I am not practicing what I would like to
> do, but I am doing the very thing I hate.

—Romans 7:15

"I used to date destruction, but now we broke up." It's a lyric by Lecrae, a Christian rapper. He goes on to explain how he has experienced a rebirth because of Christ. It's true our flesh is that bad, that desperate. Our old self in a matter of time is doomed for destruction. For some it can be in the form of twenty years, for others it's in 0.3 seconds. The old self will eventually destruct and end in eternal death apart from God.

> So we too might walk in newness of life. For if
> we have become united with Him in the likeness
> of His death, certainly we shall also be in the
> likeness of His resurrection, knowing this, that
> our old self was crucified with Him, in order
> that our body of sin might be done away with,
> so that we would no longer be slaves to sin.
>
> —Romans 6:4–6

Before I was aware of what Jesus's cross meant, I was dating destruction. We had a great time—many great late night chats, walks on the beach, parties we attended with other "old" selves, just a lot of great times one might say. Nevertheless, after Christ met me at *the well* He chose for me—well, I had to make a choice. Keep dating destruction or break up with it? I have chosen to break up with it. However, it's like an extremely haunting ex. You never know when it's coming. That is why God tells us to stand firm in our faith, and that faith comes from hearing the Word of God. Without the Bible, we've got nothing. I don't know how many times I have to tell myself that, or anyone else, but really, we have nothing without the Word of God. The Word of God is the one true standard, the true measuring stick. It's the stick that all other beliefs should be measured by. The Bible is the mind of our Lord and Savior.

A good friend advised me to dive into the book of Psalms, because David got results when he cried out to the Lord.

The man after God's heart communicated with God on a very intimate level. Through music, through lyrics, the Lord revealed His comfort, compassion, mercy, and grace to King David.

> Hear my cry, O God 'give heed to my prayer.
> From the end of the earth I call to You when
> my heart is faint; Lead me to the rock that is
> higher than I. For You have been a refuge for
> me, A tower of strength against the enemy.
> Let me dwell in Your tent forever; Let me
> take refuge in the shelter of Your wings.
>
> —Psalm 61:1–4

> Incline Your ear, O Lord, and answer me;
> For I am afflicted and needy. Preserve my
> soul, for I am a godly man; O You my God,
> save Your servant who trusts in You. Be
> gracious to me, O Lord, For to You I cry all
> day long. Make glad the soul of your servant,
> For to You, O Lord, I lift up my soul.
>
> —Psalm 86:1–4

Borrow King David's praises and complaints, and develop that intimacy with Christ. Little by little, that dating game with destruction will slowly dissipate. It will still be there in all reality; however, it will lose the power it once had over you. You will see it and know it's wrong. You will know when it's coming and what scripture you need to stand firm while it's around. The Word of God is energy, power, and fuel for our new nature.

For the word of God is living and active
and sharper than any two-edged sword, and
piercing as far as the division of soul and spirit,
of both joints and marrow, and able to judge
the thoughts and intentions of the heart.

—Hebrews 4:12

He sent His word and healed them, And
delivered them from their destructions.

—Psalm 107:20

I used to date destruction, but now we broke up!

—Lecrae

# CHAPTER 16

# COUNT YOUR BLESSINGS

## December 31, 2011

"*We* are to be about our Father's business." That was the slogan for our royal family members this year at church. That is what Jesus told Mary and Joseph when they were looking for Him at age twelve when He was found at the rabbi's temple.

> When they saw Him, they were astonished;
> and His mother said to Him, "Son, why
> have You treated us this way? Behold, Your
> father and I have been anxiously looking for
> You." And He said to them, "Why is it that
> you were looking for Me? Did you not know
> that I had to be in My Father's house?"
>
> —Luke 2:48–49

God truly blessed me and my royal family church members this year. For me personally, He kept His promises found all over the Psalms and prophets, "If you seek Me, you will find Me when you seek me with all your heart."

Every year that passes, I have a farewell motto. This year it's "count your blessings." I've told everyone I've had a chance to, wrote it on every Christmas card, yet I myself have yet to count my blessings. So here goes.

One of my goals this year was to read the Bible all the way through, and by God's grace I did. I came to meet my relatives such as Abraham, Sarah, Jacob, Isaac, Joseph, Ruth, Naomi, Samson, Esther, Mordecai, Hannah, Samuel, Job, Saul, David, Jonathan, Daniel, Isaiah, Nehemiah, Elijah, Jonah, Habakkuk, Matthew, Mark, Luke, John, some naked dude, Stephen, Paul, Peter, John the Baptist, and of course my Lord and Savior Jesus Christ. All I can say to wrap up my time spent in the Bible this year is what a mighty God we believers serve!

I decided to get out of credit card debt this year. The principle I used was that God gives and He takes away. The money I earn at work in essence belongs to Him and it's entrusted to me for a little while. That awareness helped me to control the way I spent the money God entrusted to me. I learned that God at times blesses with money. It's like a little token of His tremendous blessings. We all should take the money God gave us to His throne room and ask Him what He wants us to do with it. This past July, God Himself got me out of credit card debt in a way that is not humanly or financially possible. I didn't get a major promotion. I was deep into borrowed money from the government. A Christian financial coach pointed me in this direction:

> "Shall we pay or shall we not pay?" But He,
> knowing their hypocrisy, said to them, "Why
> are you testing Me? Bring Me a denarius to look
> at." They brought one. And He said to them,
> "Whose likeness and inscription is this?" And
> they said to Him, "Caesar's." And Jesus said to

> them, "Render to Caesar the things that are
> Caesar's, and to God the things that are God's."
>
> —Mark 12:15–17

I finally understood that God wanted me to pay my debt back to its rightful owner as it's the right thing to do. With His help, all things are possible.

I started the Broken Bones Ministry this year, an online ministry to encourage people to start their journey with Christ. I decided to use our technology today as a tool to give out His Word to my family and friends that I keep in contact with via e-mail.

God allowed a friend and I to encourage the ladies at a nursing home, where we had an hour-long Bible class. Little did we know, God was using us to bless others with His Word, and He was using others to bless us in return. The feeling you get from being able to share the hope that lies within you is an amazing feeling indeed.

I learned to praise Him in both adversity and prosperity this year. This most certainly can be a hard thing, because sometimes we get wrapped up in the good stuff, and we forget to say thank you. Remember the ten lepers who were all healed, yet only one came back (Luke 17:11–19)? We must praise Him when times are looking foggy and when hope is unseen. Praise God in all things and in all areas.

I realized again and again that God loves my biological family and friends more than I could ever love them. He knows each and every one of us so intimately. He is the Transformer, and I am merely the seed planter. I've seen it in my family and friends' lives, even though they have not. God is taking care of them with or without me, and that gives me great comfort to rest and continue my journey with Him, not necessarily worrying about their salvation, but simply praying for it.

I learned that He must increase and I must decrease, which ultimately means I need to get out of His way. I've learned that with much knowledge and grace comes testing. God has to purify us, correct us, and mold us into the person He wants us to be.

I relearned that my pastor isn't perfect. He is by nature, a sinner like me and his battles are probably more intense than mine simply because of his calling.

I learned that Psalms and Proverbs are medicine cabinets for the sick, and necessary for healing.

I learned grace means dependency on God—that God gets all the credit, as He is holy, righteous, and just.

I learned that adversity is inevitable, but stress is optional. I am in control of seeking peace and pursuing it. There is actually a lot that I can do to bend my will to meet His.

For, "THE ONE WHO DESIRES LIFE,
TO LOVE AND SEE GOOD DAYS,
MUST KEEP HIS TONGUE FROM EVIL AND HIS LIPS
FROM SPEAKING DECEIT.
"HE MUST TURN AWAY FROM EVIL AND DO GOOD;
HE MUST SEEK PEACE AND PURSUE IT.
"FOR THE EYES OF THE LORD ARE
TOWARD THE RIGHTEOUS,
AND HIS EARS ATTEND TO THEIR PRAYER,
BUT THE FACE OF THE LORD IS
AGAINST THOSE WHO DO EVIL."

—1 Peter 3:10–12

Last, I learned that I still have a lot to learn! God simply out blessed and out graced me by going above and beyond what I had in mind for the year. I know the only reason is because I was seeking for Him. When you seek God, He will reveal His love, power, grace, and justice to you and your life will start to change.

I pray that 2012 will be a tremendous continuation of growing in God's grace and knowledge. I pray that the rooms in your souls that have yet to be cleaned will get cleaned out this year. I pray that God's timing is present in all our lives. I pray that all will count on the Author and Perfector of our faith. I pray that all will learn the true meaning behind the cross and our Lord and Savior Jesus Christ. My final verse for 2011 and to carry on through 2012 is the following:

> Do you not know that those who run in a race all run, but only one receives the prize? Run in such a way that you may win. Everyone who competes in the games exercises self-control in all things. They then do it to receive a perishable wreath, but we an imperishable. Therefore I run in such a way, as not without aim; I box in such a way, as not beating the air; but I discipline my body and make it my slave, so that, after I have preached to others, I myself will not be disqualified.
>
> —1 Corinthians 9:24–27

# CHAPTER 17

# ARE YOU A DISCIPLE?

## January 13, 2012

*O*ne day when you have nothing to do or when you purposely do not want to do anything, try this at home. Stay in the dark for an hour or two if you can. All dark, pitch black and just dwell in that moment. After the time is up, turn the light on.

The result is exactly the pattern that happens to our souls and minds when we live in sin. I think this is a great exercise to do in order to see and grasp the difference between darkness and light. Our flesh resides in darkness. We enter into the danger zone when we can't discern the difference between darkness and light. This is apathy and carelessness. This is compromising the Bible's guidance. This is disobedience to God's instructions for us. Do you know what He calls His disciples?

> You are light to this world. A city
> on a hill cannot be hidden.
>
> —Matthew 5:14

One may think, well the light isn't shining on my end of things right now. Well let me tell you, we have no light solely "on our end of things." We have no light without Christ. Christ is the Light. Christ is the Word of God therefore the Word is our Light.

> He is clothed with a robe dipped in blood,
> and His name is called The Word of God.
>
> —Revelation 19:13

> Your word is a lamp to my
> feet And a light to my path.
>
> —Psalm 119:105

It takes time to train your mind. It takes obedience to get it done God's way because God is a precise God. He never changes. He is the same yesterday, today, and forever (Hebrews 13:8). If He sets standards, He will not budge. We can't sweet talk Him into changing His plans. Yes, He loves us, but He has no problem disciplining us and telling us how we should follow His ways. He tells us clearly how to walk in His ways by His grace for His name sake through His written Word, His very own mind. Darkness is your flesh's decided path; light is the new nature's God-given path.

> If Christ is in you, though the body
> is dead because of sin, yet the spirit is
> alive because of righteousness.
>
> —Romans 8:10

It's only because Jesus lived and died for us, and started this new spiritual race, that we are now called sons of the day, children of the light (1 Thessalonians 5:5).

We have been sanctified in Christ, set apart because of the blood of Jesus. Therefore, we have been enlightened. We ought to shine brightly because of Him. We ought to discipline ourselves into learning the Word of God (our manual while sojourning here on planet Earth) because of Him. We ought to spend some time to see how God wants us to walk, see how He wants us to talk, see what He wants us to do with the time, talent, and treasure He so graciously entrusted to us because of His strength in our newness, nothing of our own. We need to find out what's up! Why are we here? Why didn't God just take us home after the day we trusted His Son, the King of kings, our Lord and Savior Jesus Christ? We can only produce light in our new nature with the mind of Christ. It's His light that is shining, not ours. It's He who is guiding us, not us leading ourselves.

God manifested Himself to the Israelites who were part of the Exodus troop by guiding them as a pillar of fire burning brightly at night. The wise and humble shepherds were led by a bright star to Bethlehem. Now we Gentiles have that star in us through Jesus's resurrection, therefore producing His very same light through us. What should we do with this light, or what is the purpose of this light? To hide it? May it never be. It's to glorify our Father. Through Jesus we now have His light.

We have been left behind here on planet Earth for a little while, burning brightly, and elevated as a city on a hill and as His mind so beautifully state's "a city on a hill cannot be hidden." His light should shine bright—as bright as that initial reaction when you turned the light on, after being in the dark for an hour or so.

Disciples equal discipline.

Discipline equals disciples.

Disciples equal His light.

This is why Jesus told us we are lights of the world. Better find out why you are a light, how you got it, and what you are to do in it. All I know is this: "No one, after lighting a lamp, puts it away in a cellar nor under a basket, but on the lampstand, so that those who enter may see the light" (Luke 11:33).

# CHAPTER 18

# HEAVENLY PLACEMENTS

### March 3, 2012

*I*'m sure a lot of you are familiar with Mercy Me's song "I Can Only Imagine." This song gets me emotional every time I hear it. Why wouldn't it or why shouldn't it? Let me propose one thought to you. Whether you care to believe or not, there will be two judgments after your body passes away from this earth. The first judgment is the white throne judgment (Revelation 20:11–15). The second judgment is known in the original languages as the bema seat judgment (2 Corinthians 5:10).

The first judgment is simply based on belief in Christ paying for your sin, and acknowledging Him as Lord in your life.

> "Sirs, what must I do to be saved?" They said, "Believe in the Lord Jesus, and you will be saved, you and your household."
>
> —Acts 16:30–31

While going through my fourth toll, driving six hours up north to visit my parents, I painted this picture in my mind. Imagine the first toll gate as the white throne judgment. It will only have two lanes—one lane if you believed in Jesus Christ and the other if you did not. One lane will take you to heaven; one lane will take you to hell. This judgment is crucial for the person who chooses not to believe.

Has God sent someone in your life to give you His Word? Has God changed someone you've known for the better? Has God come through for you even when you didn't quite believe He existed? Have you ever had everything go wrong, yet you were still alive? Have you witnessed a woman give birth? Have you carried a baby straight from the womb? Have you ever helped someone who was in need? These are acts of God. God is real, and God is alive. He doesn't merely watch on high to take records of all of our shortcomings. He is not pleased with our definition of morality. Morality doesn't produce spirituality; spirituality rather produces morality.

> Therefore the Lord longs to be gracious
> to you, And therefore He waits on
> high to have compassion on you. For
> the Lord is a God of justice.
>
> —Isaiah 30:18

Unbeliever, please listen. There will be a day of judgment whether you want it or not. It's going to happen; it's pretty much engraved in stone. God is a loving God, which is why you are still alive, which is why He has sent His love for you through people, places, and everything in between. His Son dying on a cross was just for you. He wants to have a relationship with each and every one of us. Yet so many of us don't want to have a relationship with Him. So many of us say we are sinners and are not worthy of God. Some say if I go to church, it will surely burn down. Well if that were the case, the whole earth would have burned down years ago. Do you know what is highlighted all throughout the Bible? The fact that we are sinners. Think about this for a minute. If the Bible was written by men, why would they write about their shortcomings, their failures, their sin, their evilness? I know I wouldn't. I would find a way to exalt myself. I wouldn't write that I was an adulterous or a murderer like David and Paul had to profess. Why would anyone want to highlight their failures? This should tell us that the Bible had to be inspired by a supernatural being. A human would not highlight the problem. We don't like problems. We'd rather not bring them up again, let alone have them established in a book that's over six thousand years old—a book that many people will read over and over, and the only book that is available in jail cells. No wonder so many jailbirds become free even though they are behind bars. God knows what He is doing. God loves you; He is waiting for you to choose to have a relationship with Him. He wants you exactly how you are, because He *knows* exactly how you are. How many people have you heard say that even at their darkest hours, they knew someone was watching over them? That someone is God. That is His true nature, confirmed over and over in the Bible. If one will not take the time to read the Bible and find a pastor who can reveal all the white spaces within the Bible, one will never know there is a God who created them exactly the way they are. The same God redeemed them, if only they accept His solution that unfolded on the cross that beautiful day when Jesus yelled, "Father, forgive them for they know not what they do" and "It's finished!" The sin is finished. All of humankind's sin has been forgiven by one act: Jesus Christ dying on the cross. It's devastating to see that many religions today fail to take notice of the power behind the cross. It's devastating to hear so many people speak about their faith, yet have no clue why Jesus died on the cross. Trust me, I was one of those people.

Two lanes, either heaven or hell is the final destination. Once the hell lane goes, it's gone. Absolute misery, forever and ever. You know how fairytales end with "and they lived happily ever after"? Well hell is the exact opposite.

> And will throw them into the furnace
> of fire; in that place there will be
> weeping and gnashing of teeth.
>
> —Matthew 13:42

Hell is not going to be pretty. Ever hear people say, "Oh I'm fine with going to hell"? What an ignorant statement. If one knew what the Bible said about hell, one would not wish that on anyone, let alone being comfortable about going. The number one misconception this day in age is that sins take people to hell. If that were the case, we would all be in route to hell. The thief on the cross was able to get to paradise/heaven that day because he believed that the man to his right was His Lord and Savior. That blameless man Jesus Christ took his sin and died for him as the ultimate sin offering.

> One of the criminals who were hanged there
> was hurling abuse at Him, saying, "Are You
> not the Christ? Save Yourself and us!" But the
> other answered, and rebuking him said, "Do
> you not even fear God, since you are under
> the same sentence of condemnation? And we
> indeed are suffering justly, for we are receiving

what we deserve for our deeds; but this man
has done nothing wrong." And he was saying,
"Jesus, remember me when You come in Your
kingdom!" And He said to him, "Truly I say to
you, today you shall be with Me in paradise."

—Luke 23:39–43

In the Old Testament, they had to find spotless animals
without defects to offer to cleanse them of their sins. This
was a foreshadow of Jesus. He was the ultimate sin offering
(Leviticus 4:3).

The other lane leads to heaven. Ah, heaven. But before we
enter heaven, there is yet another toll gate. This time this one
has multiple lanes, more than one can count. Whoa, why so
many lanes in heaven, one may ask? Well look at the parable
of the talents found in Luke 19:12–28 and Matthew 25:14–30.
I won't write it all in here. Please open the Bible and read
for yourself. This toll gate can be compared to the second
judgment. It's a judgment of believers only. What will this
judgment encompass? It will assess what we did in our flesh
that brought glory to God. To put it simply, after we chose to
believe in Christ, what did we choose to do next? *Eek*, this is
where it's going to get ugly for some and beautiful for others.
Now remember, the choice is yours. What you decide to do
with what God has given is totally up to you. If you think
otherwise, let me ask you something. When was the last time
someone controlled your mind, without you giving him or her
permission to? That's what I thought. We control our mentality,
which is where we love God from first. Our mentality is our
stabilizer. Mentality turns into action. Whatever is on one's
mind will eventually come out through one's body motions.

Everyone who competes in the games exercises
self-control in all things. They then do it
to receive a perishable wreathe, but we an
imperishable. Therefore I run in such a way,
as not without aim; I box in such a way, as not
beating the air; but I discipline my body and
make it my slave, so that, after I have preached
to others, I myself will not be disqualified.

—1 Corinthians 9:25–27

Do you really think a just God would reward the following two persons with the same prize? A believer since January of 2001 decided to not be a disciple. He believed, but he went back to the world's association. He didn't read the Bible. He only went to church on Sundays for an hour, and then the rest of the time he was out doing everything but learning God's Word. On the contrary, a believer since January of 2001 since then has made every possible effort to develop a more intimate relationship with Christ through His written Word. This person fell of course, because we are human. We all fall, over and over again, but this person got up after multiple falls and kept going. This person ran the race and got tired at points. Some of those points lasted for months and years, but he kept going by agreeing with God that he sinned and acknowledging his sins to God along the way in private, which then enabled him by God's strength, to remember his position in Christ and continue on. Do you really think these two believers should have the same heavenly placement in heaven? If you have no desire to want to live with God now while you're on earth, why would you expect to know how to live with Him face to face in heaven?

The people who went through the heaven lane, because they believed in Christ at one point in their life, will now get judged by what they did with their faith in Christ. Did they put their faith into action, or did they simply take it and run back to the world, forgetting all about it? The good thing is that God is so gracious. At least they will be in heaven, meaning they will be perfect and happy, but God's going to show them what they could have been.

> For no man can lay a foundation other than the one which is laid, which is Jesus Christ. Now if any man builds on the foundation with gold, silver, precious stones, wood, hay, straw, each man's work will become evident; for the day will show it because it's to be revealed with fire, and the fire itself will test the quality of each man's work. If any man's work which he has built on it remains, he will receive a reward. If any man's work is burned up, he will suffer loss; but he himself will be saved, yet so as through fire.
>
> —1 Corinthians 3:11–15

God's going to show us what we could have been, if we would have allowed Him to rule our lives on earth. At some point, think about the following four questions:

> Do you believe that Jesus Christ died on the cross for your sins once and for all, never to bring up the sins again?
>
> Did you note that neither of the judgments were sin based?

If you have believed in Jesus Christ, what are you doing with the time, talent, and treasure God entrusted you while sojourning here on earth?

And last, the most popular question the world offers in my opinion is this, "What do you want to be when you grow up?" Well let me tell you what the most important question is in all reality, as this world is going to pass, and so are we:

What do you want to be when you get to heaven?

If you want to be a king in heaven, you better find out how by reading the Bible and finding a pastor who will teach you the wisdom of the Bible. If you want to be a "pauper" in heaven, fine. I pray God will reveal to you how to improve right now before judgment comes and to reveal to you your true potential. I quote an unknown person when they asked, "Do you see U-Haul trucks at funerals?" Definitely not, because we can't take anything we've accumulated here on earth during our sojourn.

I know what I want to be, so that's what I am striving for. I want to hear what the master told his slave in the parable of talents when I meet my Lord and Savior face to face, and I hope many of you do as well:

> His master said to him, "Well done, good
> and faithful slave. You were faithful with a
> few things, I will put you in charge of many
> things; enter into the joy of your master."
>
> —Matthew 25:21

Surrounded by Your glory, what will my heart feel? Will I dance for you Jesus or in awe of you

be still? Will I stand in your presence or to my
knees will I fall? Will I sing hallelujah, will I
be able to speak at all? I can only imagine.

—Mercy Me

Let's stop imagining what we will be in heaven for a moment, and let's pray and get some much-needed guidance while we are still sojourning in time, on earth. Because heaven is eternal, people, whether you like it or not. It's everlasting. Wouldn't you rather be a somebody in eternal heaven, rather than a somebody on temporal earth?

I have fought the good fight, I have finished the
course, I have kept the faith; in the future there
is laid up for me the crown of righteousness,
which the Lord, the righteous Judge, will
award to me on that day, and not only to me,
but also to all who have loved His appearing.

—2 Timothy 4:7–10

# CHAPTER 19

# MORALLY GOOD, SPIRITUALLY GONE

## April 5, 2012

$\mathscr{I}$f I could do this. Only if I did that. I will start tomorrow. I can't go to church; I have to stop drinking first. I have to stop having premarital sex. I do so much good for people. I'll do what I feel is right. I haven't killed anyone. I haven't stolen anything. The list of human "good" and "bad" goes on. The Pharisees and the Sadducees had it wrong. Morality is what our eyes see. Spirituality is what is hidden from our sight tangibly. What exactly is morality?

Moral: pertaining to right conducts or duties, discriminating between right and wrong; ethics.[7]

Having the ability to choose is what makes us human. Adam and Eve were created trichotomist beings; they had body, soul, and spirit. They were in perfect unity with the Lord in the garden until they ate of the tree of the knowledge of good and evil, which I'll call "morality." They partook of

---

[7] *Webster's Dictionary*, 1987 ed., s.v. "moral."

this tree, which killed their spirit (which is from God) and left them with only body and soul. This is why God told them not to eat of this tree, because if they did they would surely die. However, they did not "die" right? Well, a part of them did; they died spiritually, leaving them with the body (the casing) and the soul, which has the ability to choose morals.

We of course derive from Adam and Eve. Therefore we come into the world as dichotomist beings, having just body and soul. We are born without the spirit, which is why Jesus told Nicodemus one must be born again. We must be spiritually born again because humankind lost their spirits in the garden on Adam's behalf. Once you believe in Jesus Christ as your Lord and Savior, you become whole once again as Adam and Eve were prior to eating of the tree of "morality."

Morality is something any human can do, something we are automatically born with. If someone was on the road dying and you drove by, would you stop? Does that mean you're spiritual? Not really because I'm pretty sure most atheists who don't believe in God would do the same thing. To be moral is to simply be human. Spirituality happens when Christ comes into your life. Why Christ? Because the fruit of the tree of the knowledge of good and evil was sin. God wants nothing to do with sin. Sin can't stand before Holy God. Holy God is perfection; sin is disastrous.

So, what did God do to fix all of this? Well, He chose to deny part of Himself, and to come down as a human in the form of man, our Lord and *Savior* Jesus Christ. I emphasize Savior because *He saved us*! From what, one may ask? From dying. Sin would be the end of us. We can't live with God in sin. He is holy; sin is not. God had to make us holy again so we could have communion with Him.

I am the way, the truth, the life; no one
comes to the Father except through Me.

—John 14:6

When you believe that Christ is your Savior, Lord of your
life, you become acceptable to God because Christ's death on
the cross was sin's very death. Sin was destroyed when Christ
died, because Christ was made the ultimate sin offering.

But God demonstrates His own love toward us, in
that while we were yet sinners, Christ died for us.

—Romans 5:8

It's simple yet hard to believe, because our human minds
always want to be a part of the solution. We are the problem
so we can't be part of the solution. In our case our solution had
to be outsourced. Christ was the solution. Sin in humankind
was the problem. Christ died, sin died, "it's finished." Now
all one has to do is believe it. That's how to get to heaven and
live eternally peaceful with almighty God. Morality will not
take us to heaven. If that were the case, why is King David
there? Why is the apostle Paul there? Why is the thief on
the cross there? Why am I going there? Because the solution
takes us there. Believe in the solution and live eternally with
almighty God, like the days in the garden. I know, this debunks
everything we've been taught growing up, but it's not about
being good or bad at all. We were born sinners in God's eyes
without Christ, yet He still loves us anyway and waits patiently
on high for us to come to this knowledge of His love.

Therefore the Lord longs to be gracious
to you. And therefore He waits on high

to have compassion on you. For the
Lord is a God of justice; How blessed
are all those who long for Him.

—Isaiah 30:18

Our God is such a patient, loving, and gracious God. Even though humankind continues to reject Him, His door is still open and will remain open until the trumpet blows. Belief in Christ is the ticket to eternal life. Stop saying, "Oh I'm good. I haven't killed anyone. I do what is right." All that is correct, why? Because you are a human and you have morals. But always remember morality doesn't get you to heaven. Faith alone in Christ alone is what is going to carry you there once this world comes to an end.

# CHAPTER 20

# LOVE CAME DOWN
# AND RESCUED ME

### July 28, 2012

*W*hat Satan failed to miss was this: Christ resurrected on the third day, and when that happened God gave each and every believer in Christ, the Helper, His Holy Spirit. The Holy Spirit's role enables us to do all things through Christ who keeps pouring His strength unto us. I want to unravel this important information in two lights that God has bestowed upon every believer. I pray it will make you more aware of who and what you are in Christ.

Light number one is the position we inherited in Christ. If one believes in the Lord as one's Savior, that person is now placed in Christ. We are fallen, sinful men until the day we obtain awareness to believe in Christ. Once we believe, the way God looks at Christ is the way He looks at us, because we have been made one in Christ. This is pretty much solid ground here, black and white, no ifs, ands, or buts about it. Once you believe, you are in Christ. Welcome!

Light number two is the experiences we have in Christ. This is where things begin to take detours. This is where every believer is different in likeness to his relationship with Christ. This is where our decisions come into play. We must decide how being called "in Christ" will affect the rest of our days here on earth. We must decide how we will respond to such a high calling He has used His precious blood to purchase us into. This is where we can say, "to each their own."

I taught this concept to the children once in my church's prep school. On one side of the dry erase board, I wrote an address, 724 Matthew Street, and I had one of the children read the verse out loud.

> Therefore everyone who hears these words of
> Mine and acts on them, may be compared to
> a wise man who built his house on the rock.
>
> —Matthew 7:24

We then drew a beautiful house on a rock-solid foundation. On the opposite end of the board was 726 Matthew Street, and I then had another child read the verse out loud.

> Everyone who hears these words of Mine
> and doesn't act on them, will be like a foolish
> man who built his house on the sand.
>
> —Matthew 7:26

We then drew a house, beautiful as it was, on sand. I then told the children a huge storm was passing through town and started ripping the two houses apart.

And the rain fell, and the floods came, and the
winds blew and slammed against that house.

—Matthew 7:25, 27

After marking the board with all kinds of lightning flashes and making rain sound effects the two houses were in horrific conditions. I explained that because 724 was built on a solid rock foundation, it was fine after the storm passed. And if all else failed, the house could be rebuilt, since the foundation was sturdy and was laid down properly. But next door, 726 had no hope, for it was built on sand. What happens to sand when anything comes its way? It simply caves in. These verses are wonderful examples of two different experiences in Christ. Both Christians were situated "in Christ." However, one experienced His calling beautifully, and the other missed out.

Our placement in Christ ought to determine our experiences in Christ. Please don't get me wrong; I am not a master at all with this, and my house gets shaken all the time. But one thing I know for sure: it's sitting on solid rock, and it isn't going anywhere! I may sin from time to time, but I know what I need to do to get back in harmony with my Lord. Some days might take longer, but I'll get there eventually. How? Because I know how much my Lord loves me. I know what happened on the cross. I understand that I have been bought with a price, His precious blood. Now it's a matter of my response to His beautiful love calling.

I was talking to a gentleman one day at the gas station as I was waiting for my inspection sticker. He said that when he realized his sin was paid for and how much God loved him, it felt like a flood coming over him, a flood of grace. That was music to my ears! Only God can produce this peace in the midst of storms. Only God, the Creator of all, can save each and every one of His creatures. Only God can manifest His fruit of His Spirit within a believer. Only God can come up with such a marvelous plan for salvation.

Max Lucado wrote in his book titled *The Cross* something along the lines of this: Jesus Christ was on the cross. God and the angels were looking down from heaven, and one of the angels asked God, "Must it be this painful?" God with compassion said, "Yes, if it isn't, it wouldn't be love." Only God could come up with that.

Assess yourself. What is your response to His love? Your response will determine your experiences in Christ. Your response will determine the liveliness that a Christian can have here on earth. My previous entry was about human morals and how none of that matters in getting to heaven. By no means did I recommend to go out there and "sin it up" once you're saved. Rather, if your heavenly Father poured this much love onto you, why would you respond by willfully choosing to continue to live in sin? His gift of grace should not warrant us to sin. Grace is a chance to respond to the one who so graciously gave. That is how we should understand grace. He just loves us; therefore, He gave.

I remember listening to Andy Stanley for the first time. He was teaching about the prodigal son. He stated that the younger son, after finally realizing what his life had become after leaving his father's estate, came up with a speech. He started to somewhat rehearse it on his way home. "What am I going to tell my father? Is he going to accept me back? Maybe he won't, I'll tell him I'll do anything, even be a servant in your home, Dad!" Then when the son got home, what happened?

> But while he was still a long way off, his
> father saw him and felt compassion for him,
> and ran and embraced him and kissed him.

—Luke 15:20

That is the love relationship God desires to achieve with His children—that personal, intimate relationship with Christ. That is what should define our experiences in Christ, due to our inheritance in Christ. When God looks at you and me, we must remember He sees Christ. How will you respond to that? Does that get you pumped up or what? Does that make you want to shout on a hilltop, run and tell all of your family members, friends, coworkers, and strangers for goodness sake?

I have met way too many Christians in the past month who are playing hide and seek. They are hiding their faith. They only speak about Him when someone else breaks the silence. I'm not sure if they are embarrassed, but they are hiding their faith. They are hiding the fact that they are positioned with Christ, and therefore they aren't experiencing Christ. Trust me, I know we all have the bad days.

I'll leave you with this as a reminder that the true light has come to shun away darkness. Your darkness, my darkness, complete darkness is no more to be found when the light enters in.

> If I say, "Surely the darkness will overwhelm
> me, And the light around me will be night,"
> Even the darkness is not dark to You.

—Psalm 139:11–12

God loves you. If you don't know Him, the light has come. Soak it in. If you think you know Him, but you don't really understand what He is all about, it's time to open His Word.

It also helps to find a church, a body of believers to help encourage you on this new path.

> Then Jesus again spoke to them, saying,
> "I am the Light of the world; he who
> follows Me will not walk in the darkness,
> but will have the Light of life."

> —John 8:12

I pray that we who know this loving God will start living in our inheritance with Christ. We can then start to truly experience what His love, power, and grace are all about while on this earth. When we get to heaven, the celebration begins.

> For this son of mine was dead and has
> come to life again; he was lost and has been
> found.' And they began to celebrate.

> —Luke 15:24

# CHAPTER 21

# LOSS OF MEMORY

## January 26, 2013

> For I give you sound teaching; Do not
> abandon my instruction. Let your heart hold
> fast my words; keep my commandments
> and live; acquire wisdom! ... Do not forsake
> her, and she will guard you, Love her, and
> she will watch over you ... Prize her and
> she will exalt you, she will honor you if you
> embrace her ... take hold of instruction; do
> not let go. Guard her, for she is your life.
>
> —Proverbs 4:2–13

*I* never thought it could happen to me. "I know myself," "when I have a goal in mind, it happens," and "I will make sure it doesn't go back to where it once was." Fooled again! My flesh is good. She is brilliant actually. Too bad she works for the other team. I could really use her tactics. She fooled me ... again, pretty much on the same subject as her last successful win.

The problem is when I start to believe she is the real me. Truth is she isn't the real me and I need to remember this. What I've experienced in the past few months is a loss of memory my friends. I forgot why I was on this earth. I forgot why I had to go through heartache and pain. I forgot that I have been bought with a price, and that I belong to God. I forgot it all. I never thought I would. I remember someone telling me to cherish that first year after the realization of salvation, because it will be hard to maintain that period and continue on. Most Christians, as they continue to walk, lose their fervency. I sure did. I wasn't the same. I wasn't experiencing Christ's highest and best, because I took a detour. I let my old sin nature take control again. I fed her too much garbage, making her grow an inch too tall to take over my mind. The reality is, it's tough here on Earth, because this other side of me, this enemy within, is of this world. When I allow her to be in control, it's all over, because this is her realm. The realm will embrace and surround her. It's very tough, however I remember by God's grace that I am in Christ Jesus. I remember I am not of this world. I remember that I am His bride, a child of God.

If you have gone through this, or if you are going through this, I urge you to cling to God's Word. The only way we will remember again is through His Word. I am not sure how I lost my memory, which raises a red flag for my new nature. If I can't even remember when I lost it, then that means at any time if I am not on guard, I could lose it again. My walk will not be efficient, my testimony will be shot, and my rewards will be at risk.

The one thing I do remember is that I forsook God's words. I didn't read the Bible as much as I used to. I didn't give it the attention I once did. I'm not going to lie—I didn't put it first and foremost. I want to encourage you if you are going through this. I'm telling you the truth. I went into the world. I'm sure it started with a little peek, and then a little more, and then a little more, and then—*bam!*—my old sin nature was the life of her own little party again.

What can one do if this happens? First, realize God's grace in allowing you to be convicted of this deviating heart. In prayer, thank Him, praise Him, repent yet again, and be filled with the Holy Spirit. Deviate from the old sin nature's thoughts and actions. Cleanse your thoughts with God's words. Allow His thoughts to be your thoughts. Allow His ways to be your ways. You must intake of the Bible daily, as if it were a meal. You should not skip a meal, especially this meal. And this should be the largest meal of your day. Nutritional experts say breakfast is the most important meal of the day. I challenge them and say that prayer and devotion to God's Word is far more important than earthly breakfast.

> I have not departed from the command of
> His lips; I have treasured the words of His
> mouth more than my necessary food.
>
> —Job 23:12

God is the sustainer of all. Yes, we need food for our bodies. However, our souls need food in order for our bodies to even function. What good is the body if the soul, mind, heart is weak and corrupt? Friends, we are only here for a little while. We can't afford to keep losing our memory. Yes, it will happen from time to time, but may it be a short term rather than long. The New Testament repetitively states that we are to walk in "a manner worthy of our calling." Why return to the old ways of your old sin nature? When this happens it only gets worse because the world misses one of its own. The world throws "welcome back" parties for our old sin natures. Come on, be real; your old sin nature loves to party in whatever strength or weakness he has. First it's the nature, then the body, then the mind, and then it's downhill from there.

> Therefore be careful how you walk; not as
> unwise men but as wise, making the most
> of your time, because the days are evil.

> —Ephesians 5:15–16

The warning is this: watch what you listen to, watch who you listen to, watch where you go, watch who you go with, and in general just watch out! We are on enemy grounds. We are not of this world; we are merely sojourners. We shouldn't expect to become comfortable here. This world is not supposed to feel comfortable for us who are in Christ. The only way to remember this is to keep focused on our Lord and Savior. Remember when He was on planet earth and how He walked? Remember how He spoke? Remember how He hung out with sinners yet He did not partake of any sin? He would leave to pray alone. He knew He was on enemy ground. He knew Satan was tempting Him in all things. He knew the plan. He never forgot it. I'm sure every morning, part of His prayer was, "God guide me today in this world, help Me to keep My mind focused on My calling." He did this daily and consistently for three years before His final curtain call. Without developing that relationship with His Father here on enemy grounds, He would not have been able to go through the beatings, the mockery, for He was a human just like us. He suffered all the things we could ever suffer, for our sakes.

> For we do not have a high priest who
> cannot sympathize with our weaknesses,

but One who has been tempted in all
things as we are, yet without sin.

—Hebrews 4:15

He did everything for us. He thought of us when walking with the cross on His back. He fulfilled His great calling. He never once forgot.

Now I preach that I am in Christ; can I prove that I am in Christ by my actions? Can I pick up my cross daily and follow Him? Can I deny myself every day and trust Him for the provisions? If I forget to open my Bible, if I forget to partake in the spiritual meal. If I forget my fellowship with the Holy Spirit, then I will forget the reason I am here. It happened to me, friends. However, when I remembered, it was a moment of pure celebration. Remember, God will never leave you or forsake you; He will never give you more than you can bear. Don't *ever* forget that. Don't forget His promises; hold on to them, for they are life. Choose life that you may live … again and again. Repent and continue, continue and persevere, persevere to celebration. One day, there will be no more suffering, no more heartache, no more pains, no more doubt, no more anxiety attacks, no more worrying about the future, no more Satan … one day it's going to happen. Don't ever forget these things.

**CHAPTER 22**

# A MURDERER IN DENIAL

## February 24, 2013

The more and more I ponder salvation, the more I realize that conviction must come before salvation. The person being saved must come to the truth of his dying state.

Once upon a time I truly lived life thinking there was nothing wrong with me, that I had no evil resident within. I remember every decision I made was about me. I was in love with myself, whether I wanted to admit it or not. I truly didn't care about anyone except for myself. Even with boyfriends, ultimately, I didn't care about them. I only cared about myself and what I got out of the relationship. Perhaps that is the most detrimental state a human can be in. If one doesn't think one is wrong in any area, then of course one will not turn to the right. If where you are in life doesn't point to death, then you will not know where to turn for life. The truth is we are sick without Christ.

Remember what the jailer asked Paul and Silas in Acts 16? Do you see his honest question? "What must I do to be saved?"

The problem lies in that question. We tend to think there is something we can do in every situation. In reality, it's about what you can't do. If you were in a car accident and were stuck between the car and the road, how could you possible help yourself? Imagine saying to yourself at that moment, *What must I do to be saved?* There is absolutely nothing you can do. This is quite the picture of salvation. There is absolutely nothing any human can do to save himself. We are sick, and we need a physician.

I remember being sick. I could barely get out of bed. How would I be able to make myself healthy again with that type of weakness? Well that is exactly how we must view salvation. We must take "we," "I," and "me" out of the equation. Many of us are thinking right now, *Well I haven't really done anything to really deserve anything less than a high five from God, so what you are saying more than likely doesn't apply to me, but thanks anyway.* Others say, "Well if you were not in the jam to begin with then you wouldn't need someone to take you out or save you, right?" That is semi-true. However, the greatest deception of our time is exactly that: Satan wants us to believe that we are okay, that we are not sick; therefore, we do not need Christ to save us. That is his whole mission. That is why you will often find yourself partaking in or with someone/something that you never could have dreamed you would have ever done. That is why God allows you to see sides of yourself you never thought you were capable of being—so you could truly see that just because you haven't killed anyone or truly harmed anyone, you are still in fact sick.

When Eve was deceived in the garden and gave the fruit to Adam to eat of it, they did actually die. Satan deceived them in saying they wouldn't die. He twisted the truth. They did die; they died spiritually. But Satan had them concerned about the death they could see, the physical death. Satan sees with his eyes, whereas God sees our minds. Satan blows the visual up. He was able to trick them and still remain true to his word in saying they would not die. But little did they know, they died spiritually. Immediately after they ate, they went into hiding from God. All are born "in hiding" from God. We have no clue of spiritual matters when we are born. That is why you've never heard a baby shout, "Hallelujah, thank you, Jesus!" when coming forth from his mother's womb. The baby is spiritually dead, which is why Jesus told Nicodemus you must be born again in John 3. You must be *spiritually* born again the Greek unravels.

Have you killed anyone? Have you raped someone? Have you gotten so drunk that you got into a car accident and killed a family? If your answer is yes to any of these, you more than likely spent time in jail. But the truth of the matter is we are all walking free prisoners. Others may not see the cell around us, but it's there. Unless you allow Christ to heal you of your sickness, resurrect you from the dead, then you are walking ... dead. Remember, Christ didn't come for the righteous; He came for the sick. Embrace your sickness so you can see the miracle that Christ only performs.

> It's not those who are healthy who need
> a physician, but those who are sick. But
> go and learn what this means: "I desire
> compassion, and not sacrifice," for I did not
> come to call the righteous, but sinners.
>
> —Matthew 9:12–13

If you still think you are good, I'll leave you with this one verse that I pray will wake you up from your deception.

## A MURDERER IN DENIAL

Everyone who hates his brother is a
murderer; and you know that no murderer
has eternal life abiding in him.

—1 John 3:15

We are all "murderers" in some way; some of us are simply
in denial.

# CHAPTER 23

# FLEETING FUN

## April 21, 2013

*I* went golfing today. It was a great time! The trees were beautiful, the company was great, and I played very well. I actually won! I picked up a worm thinking it was a twig and screamed as if I were singing a very high-pitched, long note. After golf, I went and got some tea from Starbucks because it was freezing. I came home, did the dishes, cleaned up, and stood near my water filter and realized the fun was over. I was by myself again in my apartment. There was no one to physically talk to, no one to make me laugh, just memories in my thoughts of the fun day I had. Then I wondered, *Why does the fun have to end? Why does the night have to end? Why can't I always laugh? Why can't I always have fun?*

This is exactly what earth is all about. Sure there are days when it's fun, but it will pass. Those days do not go on forever and ever. In all reality, valleys come right after the mountains. The title of this entry can very well be the definition of humankind. We are simply here one day, gone tomorrow.

Three people lost their lives in the Boston Marathon events last Monday. Several others lost body parts. One day you wake up thinking of victory over 26.2 miles, and three hours later your whole world turns upside down. I can't even imagine losing my limbs, yet there are many people who have. I bumped into a running buddy of mine at work on Thursday, and I asked him if he was at the race. He looked very sad, and said no, but he had some friends who ran but are luckily safe. He then went on to say, "What is this world coming to? People are sick." I agreed and then stated we have to turn to God. He said "I just can't right now," and I asked why not. He said, "I can't understand why God would allow something like this to happen." I then went on to explain the three wills of God that I take rest in.

God has His divine, sovereign will. He also gave humankind free will. Our free will leads to His permissive will, where He will allow ourselves to hurt others and ourselves based on our decisions. Finally, He does have an overruling will, and at any moment, if and when He decides, He can stop everything all at once.

So why doesn't He, right? Why doesn't He just stop everything already? How much more do the people on earth have to suffer? Well, it's only by His grace that He allows the clock to keep on ticking. He could have stopped it during WWI, WWII, or any other historical disaster, however He didn't. Why not? I believe by His grace, He is yet again giving many more people the chance to accept His gift of salvation through Jesus Christ and His finished work on the cross. See, the more time we have, the higher the chances are of believers increasing. That is God's grace. Sometimes these valley events happen only to remind us that a mountain is up ahead.

For His anger is but for a moment, His favor is
for a lifetime; weeping may last for the night,
but a shout of joy comes in the morning.

—Psalm 30:5

God wants us to trust Him once we believe. We must trust Him while the fun is present and when it passes. We must never be tricked into believing the fun should never end here on earth. That is a tactic used by the other team—the team that wants to steal every ounce of joy you experience, rather than allowing you to enjoy that joy, even if for a fleeting time. That team wants you to dwell on the fact that it's now gone. What humiliating power that team has to never allow us to enjoy a great moment. Thanks be to God that I realized the fun ended and knew that it was okay that it did. Tomorrow is a new day, with a whole new set of possible fun, or not. Tomorrow may be a valley. Either way, we should be content. How? Because regardless of what God's permissive will allows humankind to do, His sovereign will advises us that "there will be a day, with no more tears, no more pains, no more fears. There will be a day, when the burdens of this place, will be no more, we'll see Jesus face to face" (Casting Crowns).

We must endure God's permissive will. We must have reverence for His overruling will, and we must chase after His sovereign will. To God alone be the glory!

CHAPTER **24**

# AND THE WINNER GOES TO ...

## April 29, 2013

*T*his snippet is inspired by "the one and only." God was not joking around when He said women were the weaker vessels. I may be able to lift twelve-pound weights per arm, but I must admit I am pathetically weak.

I heard today from Dr. Charles Stanley that our flesh is the most deceiving enemy, and if I may add, possibly more deceiving than Satan himself. The flesh is deceiving because it's the mirror image of our true nature, the new nature. Our flesh is a flawed new nature and has the same talent that our new nature has. However, it's a corrupted nature, therefore corrupting the characteristics or talent God gave us. I have now named my flesh the winner in the category of "The Trickiest Spiritual Enemy."

There are three enemies found within the Bible. We must be knowledgeable and careful regarding all three, but especially the one closest to us, our flesh.

The first is Satan himself. Isaiah 14:12–14 depicts the

description of Satan. Surprisingly, folks, he is not a red-looking dragon that spits fire, or a red alien. Rather, he is extremely beautiful, exceedingly charming, and exceptionally deceiving. (Ask Eve for all the details later.) He had to have given Adam some kind of competition or else Eve wouldn't have kept going back to talk to him, right?

> How you have fallen from heaven, O star of the
> morning, son of the dawn! You have been cut
> down to the earth, You who have weakened
> the nations! But you said in your heart, I
> will ascend to heaven; I will raise my throne
> above the stars of God, I will sit on the mount
> of assembly in the recesses of the north. I
> will ascend above the heights of the clouds;
> I will make myself like the Most High.
>
> —Isaiah 14:12–14

First, he said "I will ascend to heaven." "Our Father Who art in Heaven," only holy God is located in the highest level of heaven and he wants to be right there with Him.

"I will raise my throne above the stars of God," "I will sit on the mount of assembly in the recesses of the north," and "I will ascend above the heights of the clouds." Not only does he want to be where God is, but this tells me he wants to be above God and he will not be satisfied until he is completely at the top.

"I will make myself like the Most High." He wants to be God, but we all know he can't. His only tactic is to trick or deceive people into thinking they are doing good. When really nothing without God's hand is good. These verses are Satan's very words. This is what people should think of when they deem something to be "Satanic." Something Satanic really means something that wants to be higher than God. Come on, let's get back to reality. Who or what, is higher than God; the Creator of all things? In all reality, Satan is delusional. Satanic equals disillusionment.

The second enemy is the worldly mentality. I'm going to zone in on the United States because this is the world's thinking that I personally am familiar with. This is one of the reasons I dislike listening to the news, because all it is, is a worldly recap of worldly thinking. This is why I don't log onto a Facebook account, because it's a tool that this world has come up with. These are merely my opinions. If you like to go on Facebook, go for it, but do note, be real with yourself. Eighty percent of the time I believe its uses are for human good and evil, rather than for divine good. I mean come on, give up with that excuse, "Oh I get to see people I haven't seen in a long time and keep in touch with." If you really wanted to keep in touch with them, you would have kept in touch with them pre-Facebook. Facebook is like high school all over again. Let's bring up the past, and let's live in the good ol' days when I used to be thinner and look more youthful than I do now. It's called aging! Botox isn't going to help you look more youthful. It's going to make you look like you had Botox. Have you realized that everyone who has had Botox all look alike? This is also why I can't listen to "worldly" music. The lyrics that tell me that my body looks great and gives me plenty of reasons why I should have sex with the next guy I see on the third date. Or what about the song that says I'm so lovesick, all I want to do is sit at home and reminisce of all the great times we had? What about my once-favorite song that told me I was not his superwoman, and that I will only love him in return if he treats me with respect? Talk about a feminist anthem.

The world's mentality also puts expiration dates on people.

You should be married by the age of twenty-seven to thirty-five or something is not right. Or what about the timeline of when a woman should get pregnant? Last time I read, Sarah had Isaac at the age of ninety, yes nine-zero. I love Genesis 21:2 regarding worldly timelines, "So Sarah conceived and bore a son to Abraham in his old age, at the appointed time of which God had spoken to him." Abraham wasn't a young stud either, way over the hill, that's what the world would call him. Why did God promise they would have a son at the appointed time when they were so old? Who should we believe: the world's news or the good news?

Last, as I've mentioned in the beginning, the winner of all our troubles is the flesh within us. The nature passed down from Adam—the one that wants nothing but rebellion toward God. King David prayed, "to you and only you have I sinned against." I realized this last night as I was in my flesh, wallowing away, "I don't have this, I don't have that, I'll never have that, I'll never have this" and so on as the tears flowed down my face. Next up on the batting plate was the guilt trip, "You don't have this, because you did that," yada, yada, yada. However, last night I wasn't saying the yada, yada, yada, I was crying, and I believed all my flesh's lies. "If only I could do this, if only I could stop being like this." Then the light bulb called the Word of God came on and my new nature came through for a few minutes. I was directed to pick up my Bible and start reading. I landed on Ephesians 6, which reminded me that there is a battle going on. That there is the full armor of God that I need to put on. That the battle that I have been enlisted to on the day of my salvation is not against flesh or blood, but it's against the powers in the heavenly places. I finally realized I was going about without my armor!

I went to sleep with one piece of the armor on that night, the

Sword of the Spirit, the Word of God. My flesh will continue to have power over me and doubt Bible verses every other second. However, it was not able to stop me from clinging on to them that night. This is why memorizing the verses is great, because when the battles happen at night in your bed, what better way to defeat Satan than the way Jesus did? He said, "It is written." No time to turn on the lights or Google verses. It would be a smart thing to get those verses from the new nature's memory bank.

Christ carried me and rocked me like the little baby I am until I fell asleep. The next morning, Christ woke me up and gave me another day to press on—to recall that He will never leave me or forsake me and that He goes before me, and He fights the battles for me, even in my sleep!

The three enemies do have power, I'll give them that. However, their power has no chance with Christ's power: God. I mean look at Christ at the cross, the enemy's power could not stop Him from being beaten, bruised, and pierced for our sins. Their power could not stop Him from denying His deity to die as a human while nailed to the cross. Their power was defeated that very day as Christ endured every breath and even yelled seven different sayings before He finally gave up His spirit. He didn't get killed. He gave it up for us. (Selah belongs here.)

We Christians should never fear. We should put on the full armor of God with His strength and move forward in the battle. Continue to fight the good fight until the end; until we go home, where the victory that we already have will be manifested in full. All honor and praise goes to Jesus Christ, our Redeemer, our Savior, our King, our Lord, our Power!

# CHAPTER 25

# THE SUN, THE SON, AND VITAMIN D

### June 3, 2013

*T*hree months ago, I went to my doctor's office, and it wasn't for my annual physical. Anyone who knows me knows that something must have been wrong, because doctors and Diana don't mix. The only thing I may have in common with a doctor is my handwriting.

I checked myself in because I wasn't feeling right. I was beyond fatigued. I went to the doctor, and he asked me what was going on. I gave him my symptoms, and he turned his computer on and started Googling my symptoms. He called it some program that only doctors use. However, what he came up with, I came up with myself on my computer on Google at work. He finally said, "Well, something's not right." Don't you love that? You pay a twenty-five-dollar copay to hear a doctor confirm what you already know, that something is not right.

Reason number one why I don't like going to the doctors. He concluded our ten-minute conversation and said he would order blood work to be drawn so he could see what was going on, because physically I looked fine. I got my blood work drawn the following morning, still not feeling great. I got to work and remembered I had a phone appointment with my nutritionist at work. I told her what had been going on and she told me to see if I could get the doctor to check my vitamin D level. We spoke early enough, and I did just get my blood drawn, so I gave it a shot. I called my doctor's office and asked them to check my vitamin D level, which the doctor initially didn't put an order for. My nutritionist was actually shocked that that wasn't the first thing the doctor suspected. Reason number two why I dislike doctors. Most doctors specialize in a quick fix called a prescription and are not fully educated in nutrition. Nutritionists, on the other hand, understand that what you put in your body will very much affect it.

According to what my doctor found on "his version of Google," he ordered blood work to check for the following: Lyme disease, underactive or overactive thyroid, oh and at my request, my vitamin D level. My blood work results came back and guess what? The only thing that was low was my vitamin D! Shocking, but quite interesting!

My friend did a message regarding how the stars reveal the good news of the Bible, the gospel. It's a three-part message, and the first message he introduced the largest star, the sun, and so my mind started to process this, and it reminded me of my doctor ordeal. I did not feel good at all during that time, and I couldn't figure it out. I looked fine physically to the world. No one could tell something was wrong. Kind of like a lot of people today. From the outside, things look fine, which is a good reason why judging is not a great idea, but that's for another day. What is going on inside? What would we find in one another had we done some "blood work"? Well first off,

God is the only one who can order and evaluate everyone's true blood work.

Let's bring this analogy to our spiritual lives. No one can tell on the outside if you have a spiritual defect, because the spiritual is all inward. The spiritual life begins inwardly, and then progresses slowly, outwardly. So, if your spiritual life is failing, it takes a while to finally show up and catch your attention. Usually God has to allow a physical defect to pass through, so that we can finally feel and understand our deficiency. Back to the gospel written in the stars. The sun is the largest star. Christ is the Son. Do you see where I am going? How does one get vitamin D?

It is one of the vitamins that are impossible to get simply by eating food. One almost always has to take a supplement. However, vitamin D's biggest source is the sun! Twenty minutes a day in the sun will get us the daily dosage of vitamin D our bodies need. It can't just be an exposed face either; it needs to be more of your entire body in order to really get it. SPF protection also should not be present when getting the vitamin D for those twenty minutes. I ask you to do the research on this vitamin, it's almost like a linking vitamin. It is needed in order for other vitamins and minerals to perform at their peak. Magnesium, vitamins A and K, zinc, and boron are a list of other vitamins and minerals that rely on vitamin D. Everything works better when your body has its daily dose of vitamin D.

If Christ is the Son, then He is how we get our vitamin D! Without vitamin "doctrine," all other things will not be right. Doctrine simply implies the Holy Bible or His Word. Many Christians confess they love and believe in Christ but deny the daily intake of His Word. Sooner than later, you will find yourself checked in to some type of worldly hospital, getting instructions from a doctor who just wants to give you the quick fix in ten minutes for twenty-five dollars.

When we do not intake doctrine or the Word of God daily as Christians, things cannot work properly. I attest to this. I've gone through a period in my life where I made doctrine my number one priority. It cost me a lot of tears. It cost me my social life. It cost me certain friends and family members. It cost me a lot according to this world. However, that time was the best time of my life! I was so content, even when things didn't look so great. I was still content, living every minute as though I was superwoman, and I can boldly say this by His grace. I was able to be content because I had my daily dose of vitamin D from the Son. I wouldn't live without it, and that is why I carry my Bible in my purse wherever I go. That was roughly a year and a half ago.

Now I'm in a period of my life where doctrine honestly isn't my number one priority, and this life is starting to wear me down. Slowly but surely my spiritual life will fade if I do not stop and recall what God has placed in front of me, His Word, which is to be looked upon daily. Without His Word, other nutrients or aspects of my life aren't performing at their peak. Without doctrine, it's simple; our memory fails us. We forget why we are here, we forget what our purpose is, and we forget everything that is godly. You know what's scary? It's a slow fade. I was suffering for a while, before I finally decided to check myself in. I did so because I wasn't feeling great physically and mentally, but what about spiritually? How much more important is the spiritual over the physical and mental? If the Holy Spirit is active within, the physical and mental become activated.

Oswald Chambers put it nicely in his devotional book, *My Utmost for His Highest*: "The disciple who abides in Jesus is the will of God, and his apparently free choices are God's foreordained decrees. Mysterious? Logically contradictory and absurd? Yes, but a glorious truth to a saint."[8]

This is a great statement for us believers when we don't know if we are in God's will. Ask yourself this—does it seem logically absurd? If so, then it more than likely is God's will. Think about it—the only way we know God is from the Bible. I've met so many people who need more proof other than the Bible, and I can't give it to them. To them it's absurd that I am trusting in this one book. But my answer to them is read it. All the people I've spoken to have read a few pages here and there, and they are fast to conclude it's absurd. Read the whole thing, and then tell me that a book that has over forty authors, sixty-six books displaying humankind's sinfulness and God's grace, in the span of who knows truly how many years is not God inspired. Mere men didn't write this book. Mere men were used as vessels because they had the eyes to see, the mouths to speak, and the hands to write, but God breathed His message to and through them. Second Timothy 3:16 states boldly what no other religious book dares to state. No wonder it's the most hated book in many nations. Shouldn't that grab people's attentions? What is this book all about? How is it that many lives have been altered for the better because of this one book? How is it that murderer Saul turned into the apostle Paul? How? Come on, someone logically explain it?

> All Scripture is inspired by God and profitable for
> teaching, for reproof, for correction, for training
> in righteousness; so that the man of God may
> be adequate, equipped for every good work.
>
> —2 Timothy 3:16–17

---

[8] Oswald Chambers, *My Utmost for His Highest* (Uhrichsville, Ohio: Barbour Publishing, 1963).

That is the purpose of vitamin doctrine. It's needed if you call yourself a Christian. Don't fool yourself. I had to stop fooling myself. Want to know what the doctor prescribed me? Anti-depressants.

God hardwired our bodies to need this one vitamin that enhances every other vitamin and mineral's role. It affects us spiritually, mentally, and physically.

> I will give thanks to You, for I am fearfully
> and wonderfully made; Wonderful are Your
> works, And my soul knows it very well.
>
> —Psalm 139:14

The sun provides vitamin D for what the physical needs. The Son provides vitamin D for what the spiritual needs.

CHAPTER **26**

# WILL THE REAL (YOUR NAME GOES HERE) PLEASE STAND UP?

## July 13, 2013

*A* friend and I went for a chat during our break at work. We had ten minutes to talk about what was troubling her. She expressed how she felt with tears in her eyes. I looked at her and saw a familiar face staring at me.

I was in her position roughly three years ago. It boggled my mind because here is this girl who I've seen many times at work with a smile on her face. I remembered her to appear calm, cool, and collected, and yet here she was speaking with me, in dire need of advice with tears in her eyes. I thought to myself, *God is so gracious, is He not?* To get us to a place where nothing really makes sense and no one can really explain why. Where fears are so loud and hope is nowhere by. Where familiar faces seem as strangers, because He wants you all alone. I told her I know what you are going through, I've been there myself, and I still battle with it every day. She was lost, confused, beautiful, she had a lot going for her, yet something was still lacking, missing is a better word. I looked her in the eye and said something along the lines of "life without Christ is not life." I told her you can try all you want to make it exciting and seem happy, but it won't be in the end. "He is trying to get your attention," I said, "and the best way to do it is through pain and suffering, because we humans are so ignorant and prideful that we can learn no other way majority of the time." Yes, there are those rare cases of humble humans, but very rare indeed. I, on the other hand, was like a black stallion, kicking and pounding as He watched over me, waiting patiently for my pride to subside.

Recently, I've been asked these questions a few times. "Why Jesus on the cross, why all that pain, and why not some other way?" When I was first asked this, I had to pause for a moment and think, why not some other way? My answer was simply, sin. Sin was that bad. Sin was the reason why we were all born separated from God. My Lord's death on the cross was the reality of sin. Jesus Christ's entire mission was to come and save the world. Save the world from what? Well remember in the garden, when God drove Adam and Eve out, they could not partake of the tree of life in the condition they were in. After they ate of the tree of the knowledge of good and evil, they were spiritually dead. God drove them out of the garden, until His prepared time when He would come down and dwell among us, in the likeness of us, in order to save us; that we would be able to partake in the tree of life. He had to kill off sin. The way He did should tell us sin was something very serious. Something that had to be dealt with in a very awesome fashion.

We tend to solely see with our physical eyes. Therefore God allowed us to see the events that led to the cross. The beatings, the crowning of the thorns, the spit in His face, the mockery, the torture, the nails being hammered into place. Yet those three hours in total darkness are incomprehensible to us. Therefore we were not able to see it.

Sin died when Jesus died. To me, this is the most misunderstood fact of Christianity. Unbelievers have yet to comprehend that their sins have already been dealt with, and are still living as slaves to their sin natures. Likewise, believers tend to forget that our sins have been paid for. May we never forget the perfect work on the cross.

Imagine this with me. Try to see yourself as sinless. I know it's hard to do, but try to imagine yourself sinless. If you can think even a glimpse of what you would be like, you have thought one tiny ray of light as to how God sees you and I. God sees us holy and blameless when we believe, because He sees Christ's saving work in us. It's only we who have yet to see the change in ourselves. We will see it in heaven when our sin natures are completely left behind.

> For now we see in a mirror dimly, but then
> face to face; now I know in part, but then I will
> know fully just as I also have been fully known.
>
> —1 Corinthians 13:12

Another question I've been asked recently has been, "If God exists, why all the pain and corruption in the world?" I again had to pause. My conclusion is, we humans more than likely need to see the worst in order to see the best. I believe God allows certain situations and circumstances to exist in order that we may see bad to understand good.

September 11, 2001, shook many people up and caused them to go to church for a season. Yet as soon as things "looked up" again, they left. In this case, September 11 was a blessing in disguise. I am pretty sure many people came to believe during this hard time. It's somewhat easier to look up when you're down. When you're up, you look around and around. God has to allow us to be down, fall, get sick, or fail, so that we can understand that we are powerless in helping ourselves get up. He has to pick us up with His strength. Oh, I used to pick myself up. I got myself up for months, even years, but when God allowed me to fall, that "turning point fall," there was no way I could get myself up. He picked me up, and all the credit goes to Him. We tend to give ourselves way too many pats on the back. If you're the opposite of my experience, we tend to look down on ourselves way too much. God at times has to do the opposite of what your own personal, human strength could do in order to wake us up.

My advice to all of you who are at this point in your Christian walk is to simply let Him in. I told my friend that day that God was knocking on the door of her soul. The very soul He created He wanted back. He wants us for Himself. He wants to accomplish something in us. He wants to glorify Himself through us. He wants to bless us, but He can't if we won't let Him. He can't if we think we are the reason we are being blessed. Let's be honest—there really isn't anything good about any of us. Try to be real with yourself for a moment. Seriously, what is good about you?

There is nothing good about me. Everything I touch turns into a mess, and everything I plan turns inward out. But with God my plans work. With God I am something. With God I am good. Actually with God I am perfect. I just can't see it yet because I'm living in an imperfect world, with imperfect set of emotions, and an imperfect physical body. But one day, one glorious day, the veil will finally and completely be torn. I will see the real me, the way He made me, the way He intended me to be. I will see who I really am in Christ.

I feel sad for those who will never see who they really were. The ones who will be in that lake of fire, because they simply said, "No thanks God, I don't need or want you." I feel sad because the Bible says, those people God already knows, and they have been judged already (John 3:18). There are many among us walking dead. They look alive, they look great in their makeup, smiles, suits, and ties, but their souls already have a spot in the lake of fire, because God already knows their answer to the great question, "What do ye think of the Christ?" (Matthew 22:42).

Tomorrow hasn't happened yet. If you are reading this, today is still here. Don't wait another day without making a choice. Answer the question, "What do you think of the Christ?"

I pray one day, you will be at the celebration and I will see you, and we will see each other the way He truly intended us to be. Until that day, will the real you and me, please stand up!

# CHAPTER 27

# NO PAIN, NO GAIN

### November 3, 2013

*〜⌒○*

Ever wonder why pain exists? Why things don't go the way you wish they would? Why would a loving God allow His creatures to go through pain? This has probably been the top question most of my non-believing friends ask, and the believers who don't do anything with their belief doubt. I recently had to go through a life-changing experience. Let's just say, as of yet, the toughest decision I've ever made. I knew what I wanted to do, but it was almost as if God was telling me otherwise, and I couldn't understand why He would ask me to do such a thing. The peaceful thing about all of this is that God knows our before, our now, and our after. He knows everything about us. He knows what we are going to choose, and He will either allow us to go through with the wretched decision or graciously hinder and alter it. I am a firm believer that He allowed me to make a very sad decision. It probably wasn't the right choice, but God knew I was going to choose it anyway. It caused me much suffering and heartache that is numbing. But I believe without it things would be a lot different.

Lately, I've been thinking about why Elijah prayed for rain so desperately. I have come to the conclusion that God knows when we are in the desert. He at times delivers us over to that desert, those dry areas of our lives, like He did Moses. Water is always connected to the Word of God in the Bible, and what do people most dread, including myself? A rainy day. It almost messes up every scheduled plan. One day I had plans with my grand-aunt to go shopping on a Saturday morning. I had a car, and she didn't want to take NYC public transportation. The plan was to pick her up, but it was pouring that morning. I called my grand-aunt and told her I didn't want to go anymore. She sternly responded, "What are you salt? You will not melt!"

How true was that statement? Why was I let down by some rain? Why was Elijah praying for rain? Then I started to think maybe rain looks bad but it really isn't. Think about it—a farmer prays for rain so that his crops will grow and be nourished. They invented a hose in order to funnel water out in case there was a drought. People spend numerous amounts of money on a water system, just look at the golf industry.

Elijah prayed for rain! I know I've said this many times, because I can't quite wrap my head around why Elijah would pray for such a party pooper called rain. I was driving home one day, and Mercy Me's song "Bring the Rain" came on, and it finally made sense to me. One of the lyrics is, "Bring me anything that brings you glory, and I know they'll be days when this life brings me pain, but if that's what it takes to praise you, Jesus, bring the rain."

Elijah knew that the state the nation was in needed some rain or else it would get burnt up. When firefighters come to quench a fire, they bring a massive amount of hoses with water pressure that could probably kill someone.

Rain is God's grace showering us. Rain is the Word of

God. How many times have you read a verse and clenched your teeth, shaking your head, "No, no way. I don't want to do it." The Word of God is sharper than a two-edged sword. Do you think it feels good to get cut? Rain is pain. Pain is grace. When Christ was on that cross, that hurt caused Him much pain. Jesus was human. Just like us, however, He didn't look human says the Bible. That's how badly He was beaten.

Not only was Christ in pain, but God the Father was in pain. Pain is grace. God gave up His only begotten Son to be sacrificed for sin. Do you think that wasn't painful for Him to see His Son on the cross? There were three hours of complete darkness between the Father and the Son that day. We have no clue what truly happened within that timeframe. I'm sure even God couldn't stand to see it anymore and so He darkened everything. That's how much pain grace is.

What about us, the receivers of grace? We too need to feel pain. We need to go through the rain. We will not melt, because the victory has already been won. That should strengthen us to stand in the rain whether it's deserved pain or undeserved. Nine out of ten times it will more than likely be deserved unless you have "arrived." God doesn't compare us to dumb sheep for no reason! He knows of all our idiotic decisions that will cause us great pain and maybe leave us in a desert situation. That's when we need to get on our knees and pray for rain as Elijah did. We must ask God to wash us all down with His high-pressured grace hose. We need the Word of God, in order to soak up the washing. We can't be cleansed without the Word. It's the most powerful thing that exists. When we pass on from death unto life eternally with God, the one thing that we will still have is His Word written on our hearts.

I'm writing this today to try to help people see God in the rain. I don't know your exact situation, but I know it's hard.

It may feel like you're all alone, but He is there. He is there like the prodigal son's father waiting to celebrate with us when we return home from our so-called adventures. All we have to do is run to Him, with open arms. He will coordinate the celebration.

I am hoping to one day enjoy the rain. I am slowly getting there. It no longer stops me from going forward with my plans, and sometimes I don't even carry my umbrella when it rains because I now know that I won't melt. That's how far I've come. But one thing I will bet on is that my God will not cause me to stumble in the rain. The rain is for my own good. Try to look at it that way in the next storm you are in. He very well could have changed the circumstance, but if you are in it, then there is a reason.

Do you remember the time the disciples encountered that storm? They had never seen something so magnificent before. Jesus Christ did not stop the storm first but first comforted them while they were going through it, and then the storm stopped. Remember that nature belongs to God, nature being the environment, as well as what's within a human's soul. He knows our nature. He knows nature. The winds and rain stop at His command. So should our pain. It should stop at His command. When He says, "Cast all your cares on Me," that's a strong command from the Mighty One. Shall we not do it then?

> I know there'll be days when this life
> brings me pain, but if that's what it takes
> to praise you, Jesus bring the rain.
>
> —Mercy Me

## CHAPTER 28

# THE CASE OF THE MISSING SNEAKERS

### May 24, 2014

It was a sad, sad day. My three-month-old Brooks Adrenaline GTS 14 sneakers were taken. I worked the nine to six shift that day to cover for my buddy. I went to the gym to work out at noon and left my sneakers outside of the café while I went to get lunch because I didn't have a bag to put them in and I didn't want them near the food. I totally forgot them as I strolled right by and headed back to my desk. My shift ended at six, and that's when I was gathering all my belongings to take them home for the weekend. I noticed my gym bag was pretty light. I realized I had left them out near the café while I was getting lunch, so I hurried right along, knowing they would be there. I got there and they were gone. I walked calmly to badge out, and in my head I knew the security guard would definitely have them at the lost and found area. He looked at me and said, "Oh yeah, they were out there for a while." I asked him, "Where are they now?" He said he didn't know and that he would put a report in the system and maybe they would show up on Monday. I left work feeling very upset that I didn't have my sneakers. I was actually going to take them to my shoe fitter to have the soles customized for my feet that weekend.

What's the whole point of this story, and how does it relate to the Word of God? It's been three weeks now, and after asking around, almost everyone I knew at work saw them, but not one brought them over to the lost and found. After the first week ended, I was still determined to find them. After the second week, I started to get angry toward all my coworkers, and then I started to get suspicious as to who may have them. When I would participate in one of the group exercise classes, my eyes automatically would check everyone's shoes out. Why didn't anyone turn them in was all I could think about. One night, the thought was tossing and turning in my mind and actually messed up my sleep. By the third week, I bought new running sneakers and decided I would move on from this ordeal.

After many days of thinking about the whole situation, doctrine finally chimed in. I reminded myself that I am living in an imperfect world right now and what comes with that are people who don't care about other people. They don't care about their belongings; all they really care about is themselves. This is probably a harsh way to conclude this ordeal, but it was the truth. The truth hurts sometimes. I have been reading Deuteronomy lately, and it states how God wants certain things handled, such as if you see your friend's ox out of his property, you are to take it and leave it at yours until your friend returns, and then you should return it.

> You shall not see your countryman's ox or his
> sheep straying away, and pay no attention to
> them; you shall certainly bring them back to
> your countryman. If your countryman is not
> near you, or if you do not know him, then

you shall bring it home to your house, and it
shall remain with you until your countryman
looks for it; then you shall restore it to him.
Thus you shall do with his donkey, and you
shall do the same with his garment, and you
shall do likewise with anything lost by your
countryman, which he has lost and you have
found. You are not allowed to neglect them.

—Deuteronomy 22:1–3

I thank my parents for teaching me when I was younger to
not steal. If it's not yours, don't take it. I'm not going to lie, I have
stolen a few things when I was younger, like lipstick, but I was
young. I didn't think the little things counted. I understand now
that if it's not yours, do not take it. If it's better to give than to
receive, then it definitely isn't better to receive by stealing, right?

On top of the book of Deuteronomy and all the statutes
listed, I have been learning in Bible class lately the human
character of Jesus Christ and how the Bible says He came to
serve, not to be served.

Just as the Son of Man did not come
to be served, but to serve, and to give
His life a ransom for many.

—Matthew 20:28

If they treated Him the way they did after seeing Him
perform miracle after miracle, why wouldn't someone take my
brand-new sneakers that cost $110?

I learned two lessons with my missing sneakers. First, it
reminded me that I am not from this world. I shouldn't love
the things of this world, because the things of this world can be
replaced. They are not eternal like heavenly things. The way

I got upset about my missing sneakers is the way I should feel when I disobey God, because that is what can't be replaced.

> Do not love the world nor the things in the world. If anyone loves the world, the love of the Father is not in him. For all that is in the world, the lust of the flesh and the lust of the eyes and the boastful pride of life, is not from the Father, but is from the world. The world is passing away, and also its lusts; but the one who does the will of God lives forever.
>
> —1 John 2:15–17

Second, this experience reminded me about that second commandment found in Matthew 22:39: "The second is like it, 'You shall love your neighbor as yourself.'" It goes back to Deuteronomy: God was teaching the Jews how to live like Him. Jesus Christ's three-year ministry on earth represented the book of Deuteronomy in action. It portrays how we are to walk as God's people. He was only here for a little while, and what did He primarily do? He served others.

What my old sin nature was trying to do was join the world's party and try to blame someone for taking my sneakers and take my eyes off Christ and put them on myself. "Poor me, someone took my new sneakers." But what I've learned by reading about Jesus Christ's life was to let it go and to care about others, not just myself. I mean in the end, they are only a pair of sneakers, and knowing God, He probably gave them to someone for His glory who needed them more than I did, and further, to show me that He has blessed me by having the means to buy new ones. We are not saved and left on this world to continue to do things our way. We are here to be conformed to the image and likeness of God Himself.

THE CASE OF THE MISSING SNEAKERS

God created man in His own image,
in the image of God He created him;
male and female He created them.

—Genesis 1:27

We are being transformed into the
same image from glory to glory, just
as from the Lord, the Spirit.

—2 Corinthians 3: 18

We are here to first love God with all our heart, soul, mind, and strength. That love will then manifest the love we have for ourselves, as well as the love we have for others. Sadly, we live in this world where it's the whole "mind your own business" mentality. This is definitely needed during certain times, but definitely not when it's a chance to display God's character to others. If someone was getting harmed publicly and you passed by, would you not stop to help? Are you the priest, the Levite who kept going, or are you the Good Samaritan who stopped to help (Luke 10:30–37)?

When someone needs something, do not deny him or her of that thing.

Do not say to your neighbor, "Go, and
come back, and tomorrow I will give
it," When you have it with you.

—Proverbs 3:28

If your child asks for bread, do you give him a stone instead (Matthew 7:9)?

The Bible says so much about how we should walk. But before you walk, you have to know how to walk. It's like riding a bike; I'm sure there are other ways to get the bike going, but someone wrote it down that in order to ride the bike correctly and safely, you ought to pedal with your feet and not your hands.

The Bible has sixty-six books that share with us what God wants from us and how to achieve it. Abraham, Isaac, Jacob, Joseph, Moses, Joshua, Samson, Balaam, Samuel, King Saul, King David, Jonathan, Solomon, Elijah, Elisha, Nathan, Job, and Daniel are only a few in the Old Testament who share with us how to walk God's walk and how not to walk during this time on earth. The ones who succeeded read Deuteronomy I'm sure. How else would Daniel have kept himself pure? He was just a teenager thrown into the Pharaoh's palace, filled with worldly temptations, but what did he do? He got on his knees and prayed, not once, not twice, but three times a day. He was taken from his country by force, yet he chose to keep God's ways.

> Now it shall be, if you diligently obey the
> Lord your God, being careful to do all His
> commandments which I command you
> today, the Lord your God will set you high
> above all the nations of the earth. All these
> blessings will come upon you and overtake
> you if you obey the Lord your God.
>
> —Deuteronomy 28:1–2

Daniel could have gotten bitter like me for two weeks, but he didn't. My sneakers were taken away; his whole life was taken away, even his name. This young man had God's statues memorized, and nothing was going to stop him from going forward—not the potential loss of his friends being burned in a fire, not the officials that were spying on him, and not even the lions! We must continue to walk in this life knowing that we are not from this world. We must continue on, knowing that there is nothing on this earth that has more meaning than Christ Himself.

> Whom have I in heaven but You? And
> besides You, I desire nothing on earth.

> —Psalm 73:25

God made it known to me the reason why I had to experience this situation. He allowed my sneakers to be taken to remind me of what's really important in this life ... Him and His ways!

> But God has chosen the foolish things
> of the world to shame the wise.

> —1 Corinthians 1:27

Lesson learned.

> Give to everyone who asks of you, and whoever
> takes away what is yours, do not demand it back.

> —Luke 6:30

# CHAPTER 29

# WATER YOU TURNED INTO WINE

### September 15, 2014

*I* think the hardest thing for me to do is to sit still quietly and wait. If you know me and have heard me speak to a customer service representative over the phone, you know it's not a pretty thing to listen to. My reasoning is, when I call the eight hundred number, I hear the robot lady and she can't make out what I really want. She goes crazy for about three minutes and finally tells me she is going to get a real human on the line. Now when the real human comes on, it's almost like I'd rather listen to the robot lady!

I used to live in New York City, and the amount of traffic in that area of the world is appalling. How can anyone want to be stuck in that? Talk about a waste of time. What about when you are at a restaurant and all is well until you put your order in and it takes about forty minutes for it to come out? I start to wonder, "Did they forget about us? Should we go and ask someone?"

I work at a golf company and started to pick up the sport in my free time. Boy, it took me a while to relax out there. When I played with someone really good, I felt like I was wasting their time with my bad shots. When I played with someone really bad, I felt they were wasting my time and I could have been practicing to get really good. I can't win is where this is headed!

Patience is definitely a virtue! It's a virtue we do not automatically have. We must choose to live a life with patience. I, on the other hand, have a problem. I can't stand waiting. It's like I'm wasting my life away. I feel like in the amount of time I am waiting, I could have done ten other things. Remember the party at Martha and Mary's house that Jesus was invited to? Remember how Martha was planning, preparing, executing, getting everything ready, and Mary was sitting at Jesus's feet, waiting for Jesus' to speak? What did Jesus conclude that evening? That Mary had it right (Luke 10:42). I remember reading that and asking myself, how in the world did Mary get it right? I guess you can call me Martha ...

Sometimes—actually, a lot of the time—Christ wants us to wait. He wants us to wait for all sorts of different reasons. Tonight, I was getting antsy about a particular situation in my life that I've battled for the past ten years. I was going to sit and watch the Food Network tonight, hoping all my thoughts would melt away after watching Guy Fieri visit all the *Diners, Drive-Ins, and Dives,* but my new nature yearned within me. I knew I needed the Word of God rather than watching the chefs cook some tasty food. I knew that the Word would satisfy me more than the Food Network.

> I have not departed from the command of
> His lips; I have treasured the words of His
> mouth more than my necessary food.
>
> —Job 23:12

I prayed as I normally do before I start reading, which I strongly encourage everyone to do. The Word of God is sacred and is God's mind. We need to get our minds in line with His mind, by clearing our minds of the fleshly thoughts so we may understand what He is revealing through His Word (1 John 1:9). If we tried to read it from our human power and viewpoint, we simply could never understand it. But if we get into fellowship with the Lord first, then we can understand what He is saying to us through His Word. I prayed about my particular situation, and I confessed how I was getting anxious about everything regarding this situation. Soon after, I opened *My Utmost for His Highest* by Oswald Chambers, a wonderful devotional. I read the day's devotional, and it surely spoke to me. I soaked it in, but I knew I missed some days prior, so I flipped back and landed on the devotional from three days ago, and there it was. The exhortation from my Lord and Savior for my current situation was written by Oswald Chambers. It's amazing how that happens. It doesn't happen all the time, but I guess it happens whenever God wants it to happen, and that is exactly what I learned again: everything happens in His time! I keep saying it because I need to keep believing it.

Oswald Chambers said this in regard to not understanding God's timing: "Stand off in faith believing that what Jesus said is true, though in the meantime you do not understand what God is doing. He has bigger issues at stake than the particular things you ask."

Wow, right? Is that a slap in Diana's face or what? If it is, it feels great! I feel alive! The majority of the time, for me anyway, He has to slap me upside my head in order to wake me up. In the beginning of my spiritual walk, I didn't like it so much. It actually hurt my feelings. I remember crying out to the Lord, asking, "Why does it hurt so much?" But I continued, stuck with Him. I persevered, and now, I kind of understand His humor. Most importantly, I understand that He understands what I need at just the right time, and He knew tonight, I needed a slap!

> My son, do not reject the discipline of the
> Lord or loathe His reproof, for whom the
> Lord loves He reproves, even as a father
> corrects the son in whom he delights.

> —Proverbs 3:11–12

God knows I know the answer to this ten-year question, because He has told me numerous times. The first time He told me, it wasn't so clear. The second time, it was still not clear, and the third time ... He could clearly see I was not getting it. After the seven hundredth time, I think I understood what His answer was, but I kept resenting it and kept fighting it. Has this happened to you? I know I'm not alone with this one. There has to be more of you like me.

I totally rebelled last year and said, "Forget it, God, I can't do it anymore! I'm doing things my way; You are taking way too long!" And what a sad, sad road I was on last year—very sad. But I turned the ship around, and I'm getting there. I'm back to the point where God has given me the same answer as before. Want to know what the answer is? He said, "Wait!" As if it doesn't get any better than that. Didn't I tell you God was funny?

Remember the word *yachal*, which is the Hebrew word for hope? It's the word used for our English word "wait" in several verses, which means "wait like we know it's coming." So, what is the problem? Why can't I wait? First, I have this flesh, this makeup that God Himself has allotted to me. He knew my biggest test in this life would be the art of patience. Second, patience is one of the fruits of the Spirit, which is actually really comforting. That tells me that in and of myself, I have no inclination of patience whatsoever, but since I have the Holy Spirit, I have a chance. Patience grows with time.

> And not only this, but we also exult in our
> tribulations, knowing that tribulation brings
> about perseverance; and perseverance, proven
> character; and proven character, hope; and
> hope does not disappoint, because the love of
> God has been poured out within our hearts
> through the Holy Spirit who was given to us.

> —Romans 5:3–5

Remember when Lazarus died? Before that Martha sent word for someone to advise Jesus that Lazarus was dying, and the Bible clearly notes that after hearing of this news, Jesus did nothing for the next two days. Then an additional two days later, He showed up at Martha's house. Lazarus was dead, and the scent proved it (John 11:6–17). We are all probably thinking, *What in the world?* Talk about Jesus not working for 911, right? I can just see Him, whistling as He was walking the long way to Martha's house. I'm pretty sure someone provided Him with some type of animal to ride on to get there quicker, but He probably refused and kept walking and whistling.

God opens our knocking doors when He wants to, not when we want Him to. He comes when He wants. He does everything in His time. The Jews who were promised wonderful things back in Genesis waited the whole Old Testament for the Messiah. Why couldn't God send Him quicker? Well, I don't think we would have an Abraham, an Isaac, a Jacob, a Joseph, a Moses, a Ruth, a Samson, an Esther, a David, a Daniel, a Josiah, a Nehemiah, a Hezekiah, a Malachi, a Matthew, a Mark, a Luke, a Thomas, a Peter, a John, and a Paul if Jesus would have come right after Adam and Eve fell.

God gave and continues to give time to His human beings, who were made in His image. Time is a blessing because without it, none of us would have a story or a reason to be. God gives us time to develop the character He blessed us with. Patience is more than a virtue, my friends; patience is God Himself. If you stop and study all the mentioned above individuals of the Bible, they all have one thing in common: they all became great, but it took some time. The same goes for you and me. We have to submit to His authority, His will, His design, and His time. If we don't, we will either be an impatient mess or an unresurrected Lazarus. Our sanctification is a lifelong process. Either we get used to His timing or we decease in ours. We have to persevere, fight the good fight, and learn to be content through both adversity and prosperity, and when we fail, we must be in harmony with God regarding our failures, and we must turn toward the narrow way. Continue to be sanctified, and may it be in God's timing, not our own.

CHAPTER **30**

# CANCEROUS

**October 11, 2014**

$\mathscr{I}$t's hard to see when it's dark. I dare not drive at night on a dark street without turning on my headlights. When nature calls at two in the morning, the last thing I want to do is turn the light on. I know my apartment in and out, so I have no problem finding the bathroom. We start to learn to see in the dark.

This principle can be applied to sin. At the first date with sin, it's pretty dark. We can't really see, and maybe we don't really want to see. As the date goes on, it gets darker and darker, but we start to develop night vision because we have been in the dark so long. With that night vision, we can see clear enough to see what we want to see, but light can't live in the dark. They are complete opposites. There can't be one and the other at the same time. Spiritually, we can't be in sin and expect to understand or grow in the light, because if sin is present, there is no light.

I know what it's like to live in the dark. I've done it, and I'm sure the majority of you can attest that you have been on the same boat as I at some point of this life. I'm not going to lie—the darkness can be fun at times, dangerous even. It's a, "What happens in the dark stays in the dark" type of mentality. But if you are a believer in Christ, there will come a point where by God's efficacious grace He will shed light around you. Either He will help you recall His promises or truths and hopefully that will be enough to get you out of the darkness for a little while, or He will call upon His saints to come help you in your time of need. He may have to repeat these steps a few times to truly get you out, but never forget this if you are a believer: He will get you out. Once you are His, you are His. Yes, He allows us to go astray, but never too far. God will fight for us. He always does, even if it is unto our death.

I've always wanted to be fought for by a man, who would lay everything on the line and fight for me. Spiritually, Jesus Christ has fulfilled this fight. I can see Him fighting for me each and every day. From the moment I wake up to the moment I lay down, He is fighting for me. Do I always appreciate it? Definitely not. Sometimes it even gets old, as if I were part of a rehearsed play. That's because the darkness has entered my soul once again. I may have picked it up somewhere along this road of life. There are so many stumbling blocks that either Satan has devised for us, we have stepped into ourselves by our own reasoning and choices, or other people's voices have directed and we have listened. We need to be careful who we listen to. The Bible says that out of the tongue resides both death and life (Proverbs 18:21). We can be a blessing one day and a curse the next depending on our soul's state. We must be very mindful and careful to take every thought captive to Christ.

> We are destroying speculations and every
> lofty thing raised up against the knowledge
> of God, and we are taking every thought

captive to the obedience of Christ, and
we are ready to punish all disobedience,
whenever your obedience is complete.

—2 Corinthians 10:5–6

A friend once brought to my attention some time ago that the Filter is Jesus Christ. We ought to filter everything through Him. If it doesn't pass His ways, especially His thoughts, discard it. Catch it with the filter, and let it go no further. This is the ongoing battle, my friends, if you are a believer. I've written this many times before. This road doesn't get smoother. It gets rougher, as if we were at sea on crashing waves rather than on a road. I love how a few of the disciples were fishermen and the majority of their lives took place at sea. They knew how calm or harsh the waters could be. I love how Jesus walked on water while it was rough. That reminds me that I have the ability to walk during the rough times because He is with me.

Sin is like a cancerous cell. It will keep spreading if left untreated. One body part at a time is given over to its deceitfulness, and we are left broken spirited because we allowed it to thrive within. Jesus Christ is like oxygen. We must breathe Him and His Word in. Cancerous cells can't thrive in an oxygenated environment. Every day we must breathe His Word in because it's our daily bread. We can't continue living sickly as believers; we must stop the cancer from spreading. We will never be healed of it completely, but we can for a brief period experience His glory. We must seek God's strength in our lives with utmost desperation. We are weak otherwise. The best thing about our weakness is that God is the mighty God. He created strength. He can take the most fragile human being and supercharge him. We have to allow Him to do it, and we need to accept His guidance in our life. We need to step out of the darkness, actually run away from the darkness. Do not flirt with it. It only gets worse, even though it may seem good for the time being. Once you are in the darkness, night vision activated, everything looks good. Beware, lest your feet stumble. Turn on the Light. Recall the verses, "The Lord is my Shepherd, I shall not want!" Tell Satan this over and over until he runs away from you. He will, but he will come back shortly.

> Be of sober spirit, be on the alert. Your
> adversary, the devil, prowls around like a
> roaring lion, seeking someone to devour.
>
> —1 Peter 5:8

I had Lasik surgery done this year, and prior to it, I thought the world was beautiful because I was nearsighted. Now my vision has been corrected and I can see all the details. The very same trees that were once beautiful can look rather frightening, because I now see all the cracks in their frame. It's the same with our spiritual eyes. We must train them to discern the beauty from the desirable. I hope this motivates you to memorize scripture so you will always be prepared. Then maybe the next time you are in the darkness, you will hear the verses you once memorized while you were in the Light.

> I will extol thee Oh Lord, for You
> have lifted me up and have not allowed
> my enemies to rejoice over me!
>
> —Psalm 30:1

Thank God for His grace! I pray you will keep on the narrow road that leads to His life for you—that abundant life the Word tells of.

Enter through the narrow gate; for the
gate is wide and the way is broad that
leads to destruction, and there are many
who enter through it. For the gate is
small and the way is narrow that leads to
life, and there are few who find it.

—Matthew 7:13–14

## CHAPTER **31**

# THE GREAT PARTY

### December 28, 2014

$\mathcal{I}$magine being invited to the best party ever. The best of the best will be there, and you will be able to speak to anyone you want to. I dare you to write your to-do list for this party and look it over. What will you wear, what will you do prior to getting there, and how will you get there? Well, my friends, this party will exist one day. You won't be able to watch it on live television; you will either be there or—be square. The great party is heaven! I cringe when people don't believe that heaven exists, because Jesus Himself spoke of it.

> In my Father's house are many dwelling places;
> if it were not so I would have told you; for I go
> and prepare a place for you. If I go and prepare a
> place for you, I will come again and receive you
> to Myself, that where I am, there you may be
> also. And you know the way where I am going.

> —John 14:2–4

Before we can get to the party, we need to answer some questions. First, why is there a party? Well, one of my favorite phrases to say is, "What is the problem?" I constantly ask this question. The problem is that everyone who can breathe has sin present in his or her body. That is the problem. The sin that started from Adam trickled down and entered into every man.

> Therefore, just as through one man sin entered
> in the world, and death through sin, and so
> death spread to all men, because all sinned.

> —Romans 5:12

In all reality, what we have is a big problem! We have a bunch of humans, including me, with this sin nature within us, and it's causing mayhem in our lives! Hence, we need a party. I don't know about you, but this sin nature, once it's gone, calls for a celebration! Can I get an amen? Sin is not just some white lie; sin is anything apart from faith in God (Romans 14:23).

Adam's original sin was his disobedience to God's words. God blatantly warned Adam that he could eat of every tree in the garden except the tree of the knowledge of good and evil. What did Adam do? Well, he disobeyed. If you dig deeper into the original sin, not only was it disobedience, but it was like a search for satisfaction. Adam and Eve were living in the garden of Eden in God's definition of perfection, yet for some reason, they were not satisfied. Satan through the serpent deceitfully convinced them that God didn't want them to eat of the tree because then they would be like God. That was Satan's original sin. He wanted to be like God.

I will ascend above the heights of the clouds;
I will make myself like the Most High.

—Isaiah 14:14

Satan used his sin to get mankind to sin. Sin is anything and everything that tries to replace God. Think about that statement for a while. That means every thought we have if it's not of faith, is sin. Our motivation, if it's without God is sin. Remember King Saul's sin before he went mad and sought David's life?

Now go and strike Amalek and utterly destroy
all that he has, and do not spare him; but put
to death both man and woman, child and
infant, ox and sheep, camel and donkey.

—1 Samuel 15:3

He disobeyed God when he was asked to destroy everything from the nation. If you are one of those people who think you are fine and you haven't done anything wrong, well, my friend, think again. A little disobedience is disobedience, regardless. You know who was one of those people? Yours truly. I thought I was just fine. I went to church, gave God an hour of my Sunday morning every week, didn't tell big lies, didn't physically murder anyone, but I did mentally commit murder according to the Bible (1 John 3:15).

You must be living under a rock to think you are not a sinner! I'm sorry to have to say it so bluntly, but at times, the truth should be blunt. Thank God, God had an invitation set in stone for us. One day in a manger a baby was born who had a mother named Mary. She was with child, yet she was a virgin.

> Now in the sixth month the angel Gabriel
> was sent from God to a city in Galilee called
> Nazareth, to a virgin engaged to a man
> whose name was Joseph, of the descendants
> of David; and the virgin's name was Mary.

—Luke 1: 26–27

An angel told Joseph, her soon-to-be, pretty much husband according to the word *betrothed* back in those days, to stick with her, even though he clearly knew that was not his child she was carrying. The shepherds saw the invitation. Even the magi followed the star. There, in that manger, a little baby was born, and they named him Immanuel, "God with us." For those of you who don't think Jesus Christ was God, His very name means God with us.

> Therefore the Lord Himself will give you a sign:
> Behold, a virgin will be with child and bear a
> son, and she will call His name Immanuel.

—Isaiah 7:14

> "Behold, the virgin shall be with
> child and shall bear a son, and they
> shall call his name Immanuel," which
> translated means, "God with us."

—Matthew 1:23

The baby boy grew up and became a man for one reason and one reason only: to invite everyone to the great party. This invitation is recorded in history by Oswald Chambers as the tragedy on Calvary. Jesus Christ dwelt among His people, both Jews and Gentiles, which sum up all of humankind for thirty-three years. On that thirty-third year, He was handed over for our sake to be beaten and crucified. He sent out the invitation that day when He yelled, "It is finished." He publicly announced to everyone that day, and many more who would later read it from His book, that if anyone will believe that He came to pay the price for our problem of sin, then we will enter in the gates of the great party. I know for certain I will be at the party, because the Bible tells me so.

> For God so loved the world, that He gave
> His only begotten Son, that whoever
> believes in Him shall not perish, but have
> eternal life. For God did not send the Son
> into the world to judge the world, but that
> the world might be saved through Him.
>
> —John 3:16–17

Jesus Christ is the invitation, my friends. He invited me sometime when I was a child; I did not clearly accept this invitation until I was much older and was reading His Word. I finally said, "Yes, please enter" and opened the door to my soul in 2011. Because of Him, I still have my health to sit comfortably on the sofa that He gave, with the money that He provided, with the job He offered, to type yet another invitation from Him to all those who wish to hear.

Jesus Christ took care of our problem. Sin no longer has reign over us. Yes, sin is still present, but it has now been rendered powerless by the mighty hand of God for us who believe. In all reality if Jesus Christ never came, then I should have been on that cross, and you should have been on that cross; there should have been many crosses. Jesus Christ stepped down from His holy status to come save us.

I'm sure there could have been a million different ways to destroy sin and save the world, but God chose the most loving way: by sacrifice. God sacrificed Himself as the Son to die on our behalves.

> But He was pierced through for our
> transgressions, He was crushed for our iniquities;
> The chastening for our well-being fell upon
> Him, And by His scourging we are healed.
>
> —Isaiah 53:5

Will you be at the great party? All it takes is a choice. All anything in this life asks for is a choice, yes or no. Let me ask you: How will you prepare for the great party? Changes will probably need to be made, because when the nature of Christ indwells our body by the power of the Holy Spirit, we can't be the same as we once were before. We will be changed. We will become more like Him, more and more each day, and one day at a time. Without the Bible, no one would know of this great party, or the invitation, or the problem. But I am part of His body, and I have now relayed His good news to you. The question now is, do you accept His invitation?

# CHAPTER 32

# TRUST ROAD

### March 18, 2016

*I* enjoy yoga because it unlocks certain areas of my body. Over the course of time here on earth, we tend to stop using certain body parts, which then locks that area and makes it tight or tense. Similarly, as we age, we tend to see, feel, and experience more hardships and stress, and it shows up in our bodies in some way or form. If we lack a certain vitamin, it will show up, whether in the outward part of our body or the inward system behind the scenes.

I used to be a runner, and I remember taking my first yoga class. I was almost in tears on some of the forward-folding movement as my body was extremely tight from all the past running I once enjoyed. That was five years ago, and since then I've completely stopped running, because to have a successful run, your stride must be absolutely correct. If it's not, you can do more damage to your body than had you not run at all.

As time goes on, I've learned a lot about my body and where I hold my stress, and where I tense up while performing various activities throughout my day. For example, take notice the next time you are washing dishes. How is your stance, what muscles are you using, and are your shoulders relaxed? I know this is starting to sound like a *Health* magazine article, but bear with me. As time moves forward, and you continue to stretch and hold poses, flexibility comes into play, and certain muscles start to lean out and relax. That's the key word: *relax*. Recently I started doing a hip routine, because I felt my hips were very tight. Come to find out as I'm doing the poses it's not so much my hips but rather my quads. They were so tense, so I started to send my breath to my quads to try to get them to relax, and I unlocked a certain area of my lower body. I shouted with joy, "Ahh, that's it!"

This is a great example of what a believer will experience in regards to his or her faith in the Lord. At first, it's very difficult to do, frightful even to put your life into someone else's hands. But slowly but surely, it will happen. I experienced a spiritual unlocking today. I know God brought me to this point in my life right now because His timing is perfect. Today, this unlocking notion hit me like no other. It happened in the shower of all places. I had a smile on my face and just shouted, "Ahh I trust you! That's it!"

This life is a journey of trust. I always pondered after salvation, why does God choose to keep us in this good-for-nothing environment? Because so much happens after salvation. Yes, the good news is you are saved, but now the trials and testing have to take place. The faith you claim to have has to be tested. God is asking us each and every day, "Do you trust Me?" And each and every day, we must answer. Now I'll be honest—there are days where I would blatantly say, "Lord, I trust You!" and five minutes later, I'd be in a corner crying, asking God, "Why, why, why?" Well that right there proves my faith has yet to be strengthened. (Then He calls me by my middle name "Peter.") I am by no means saying it's not good to cry. It's very good to cry. We must express how we feel, especially to God. He should always receive our first teardrop in every difficult, painful situation we find ourselves in. Our tears belong to Him; He knows exactly what to do with them. He will use them to wash certain areas in our life that desperately need washing. I'm talking thunderstorm, downpour, stay indoors, or your umbrella will break action.

> The way is narrow that leads to life.
>
> —Matthew 7:14

I've taken the liberty to paint the way as a road, and I've given that road a name. This is exactly what inspired me to write. On my "unlocking a spiritual journey" in the shower today, God confirmed to me that I was on the narrow road! Let me tell you how you can join me.

First, get qualified to decide which road to take by believing in the Lord Jesus Christ as your Savior. Second, pick a road, either the wide road that will lead to destruction or the narrow road that leads to life. Third, persevere as the road is truly narrow. There won't be much action on this road as far as what your eyes can see. It's so narrow that our human eyes can't keep track of it. We must use the adopted, spiritual eyes our heavenly Father has provided us in Christ. Once Christ is your Savior, you now have the ability to see this narrow road. While you are on it, you will have the strength to persevere.

Take a right onto Trust Road. Park your car, get out, and start walking. You and God alone, walking down Trust Road.

(Whistling while you walk and singing "Every little thing gonna be alright …")

They will walk and not become weary.

—Isaiah 40:31

# CHAPTER **33**

# MEN AND ANGELS AT THE CROSS

*T*here he was, bleeding, weak, dragging his feet with a cross behind his back.

"Is that a human?"

"It's the one who calls himself the Messiah. That is him."

"If he is the Messiah, why is he in agony?"

"Why doesn't he use his power and stop everything this minute?"

"I'm shocked he hasn't dropped that cross!"

"Get up, get up!"

"You, carry the cross for him!"

"The poor thing, I can't watch this anymore. Let's go."

"How will he save the world, when he can't even save himself?"

"Where did all his disciples go?"

"This can't be our savior. He is about to die."

What cruelty this world has. They actually released Barabbas and not Him. The town was in complete confusion. This man who claimed to be the Son of God didn't look like He was saving anyone. He wasn't the Messiah the Jews were expecting. He was a carpenter, who spent three years preaching and conjured up many disciples. Yes, He healed the sick, got rid of demons, gave sight to the blind, and turned water into wine, but now look at Him; He is pitiful in the eyes of man.

There He was, the mighty King and Warrior.

"He left our heavenly state to be born one of them."

"He spent thirty-three years of human life as if He wasn't the King of the universe, for the sake of those who are cursing and mocking Him."

"But many also believe that He is the King."

"Some are choosing to put their trust in Him."

"John, Mary, and Mary Magdalene have yet to abandon Him."

"Look at Him. He took all their shame, all their guilt, and bore them upon His shoulders just as He promised!"

"Yet some do not know who He is, but many will after the whole earth turns dark and the heavens quake as it receives Him back."

"Years from now, many more people on the earth will still recall this event and cherish it, because He will have His disciples write it down in the Book."

"He truly is the Lamb of God who has taken away the sins of the entire world."

"Even us, we will bow to Him when He comes back."

"He is the Mighty One."

"Holy, holy, holy is the Lord God Almighty."

"Only a little while longer, and He will return successful from His great mission: to save the world."

"We will meet the humans who put their trust in Him soon and greet them with a kiss, for they truly have shown us what faith means."

Jesus said to him, "Because you have seen
Me, have you believed? Blessed are they
who did not see, and yet believed."

—John 20:29

Then He said to me, "It is done. I am the
Alpha and the Omega, the beginning and the
end. I will give to the one who thirsts from
the spring of water of life without cost."

—Revelation 21:6

# SPECIAL THANKS

I would not have as much knowledge as I do today about the Bible if it were not from the teaching of my pastor teacher, Robert R. McLaughlin and the supplemental teachings of Dr. Charles Stanley and Dr. Michael Youssef. I hope this book encourages and reminds you all, of your great calling.

# FOR MORE INFORMATION

<u>Contact Diana Espejo:</u>

 Twitter:
@BrokenBonesDE

 Email:
BrokenBonesMinistry@aol.com

Author Website:
www.dianaespejo.com

Printed in the United States
By Bookmasters